Toby or not Toby?

That is the Question

by Martin Kayes, CISSP

Copyright © 2025 Martin Kayes

All rights reserved.

ISBN: 978-1-0369-2650-2

TABLE OF CONTENTS

1. **About This Book**
   Who am I and what do I know?

2. **The Digital Wild West**
   Understanding the Landscape of Online Threats

3. **The Psychology of Online Scams**
   How Criminals Manipulate Trust

4. **Phishing for Trouble**
   How Scammers Steal Your Information

5. **Love Gone Wrong**
   Romance Scams and Emotional Exploitation

6. **The Scammer's Playbook**
   Social Engineering Tactics That Trick Even the Smartest People

7. **Fake Websites, Scams & Spoofs**
   Spotting Online Deception

8. **Malware, Viruses & Trojans**
   How Hackers Hijack Your Devices

9. **Social Media Scams & Impersonation**
   Trust and Deceit in the Digital Age

10. **Passwords, Authentication & Identity Theft**
    Securing the Keys to Your Digital Life

11. **Wi-Fi Home & Public Networks**
    Defending Your Digital Perimeter

12. **Children, Teens & Online Safety**

Raising Cyber-Smart Kids.

13. Sextortion
Fear, Shame, and Digital Blackmail

14. Spotting Online Impersonation & Deepfakes
Do you Trust and Verify?

15. The Power of Reverse Image Search
Unmasking Fake Profiles

16. The Dark Web
What It Is, and Why It Matters

17. What to Do If You're Scammed
Recovery & Damage Control

18. Digital Hygiene
Habits of Highly Secure People

19. Hardening Your Devices
How to Lock Down Your Phone and Computer

20. The Future of Online Scams
AI, Deepfakes & Evolving Threats

21. Case Studies
Real Victims, Real Lessons

22. Your Cybersecurity Action Plan
Staying Safe, Step by Step

Foreword

"Can you recognise the signs of a scammer? Do you, or someone you know, have enough knowledge to feel safe online? If not then this book is for you."

In today's digitally connected world, your personal information, money, and identity are more exposed than ever - and online criminals know it. Every day, thousands of people are tricked, manipulated, and defrauded through increasingly sophisticated scams, from romance hoaxes to fake investment schemes, malware-laced emails, and phishing texts that look exactly like the real thing.

This book is not about fear. It's about **awareness and action**.

Written by a cybercrime and cybersecurity professional - using plain language, this is an essential guide for beginners and the non-technical alike, in understanding how modern online threats really work and exactly how to defend yourself against them.

You'll learn the tactics scammers use, how they manipulate human psychology, and what red flags to watch out for in your inbox, on social media, and in your everyday digital life.

But more importantly, you'll walk away with the skills and tools to identify risks, secure your devices and protect your accounts - responding quickly and confidently if something doesn't feel right.

No technical knowledge required. Just curiosity, common sense - and maybe a Password Manager.

CHAPTER ONE

About This Book

"I'm going to write a book to help people avoid being scammed"
- Me, 2017

I'm almost embarrassed to admit that **it has been 8 years since I started writing this book**. I'm not a slow writer - it's just that I had put the project on hold for a while whilst I relocated to London - weeks turned in to months and so on... But finally here we are.

My name is Martin Kayes, I have worked in cybersecurity since the late 1990's - back then it was mostly about securing networks and hardening server vulnerabilities - it was nowhere near as wide-reaching a subject as it is has become nowadays.

What do I know about technology and cybercrime you might ask? Well, **I hold various accreditations, including the industry-leading CISSP** (Certified Information Systems Security Professional), I am a qualified assessor for the UK Government's Cyber Essentials scheme and I train company employees in cybersecurity awareness as well as data privacy regulations (the GDPR).

I have been investigating cybercrime for over 20 years - initially that meant I was tracing hackers and fraudsters, and over time it has developed to include investigating complex romance scams and crypto fraud - and, of course, engaging with various police forces around the country.

One of my specialities is using **Open Source Intelligence (OSINT)** and **Social Media Intelligence (SOCMINT)** tools to trace and locate criminals and unmask the true identities of the people behind the scams.

But, probably the most interesting part of what I do is working with **TV production companies and the news media** to locate persons of interest, validate evidence and to appear as a subject matter expert. My work has appeared in many newspaper articles and television programmes over the years, with me even **occasionally making an appearance in front of the camera**, including on Netflix, Paramount, ITV and Channel 5.

A little bit about the book:
This book is aimed at the non-technical and people who due to their trusting nature, or lack of technical knowledge, may be prone to falling victim to scammers - I suspect we all may know somebody who could do with a little help?

As mentioned in the Foreword, the book has been written using plain language, and is intended to be an essential guide for both cyber-beginners and the non-technical alike. I have tried my best to keep each chapter short and concise, using simple language and plenty of bulleted lists, with just the right amount of information to help someone develop their knowledge, grow in confidence and be safer online.

Some of the subjects can get quite complex for what I am trying to achieve here - it would be a long and boring book if I went in to every detail of each step, such as which menu to click on and which setting to change. Instead, this book aims to give you the knowledge you need to recognise the signs (or red flags) for yourself, and what actions you can take if a scammer has their sights set on you.

In addition to this book, I have made available free **Anti-Scammer and "How To" resources** on my Real or Catfish website: **realorcatfish.com** and, for those in need of some data privacy and GDPR advice I have another free website called: **gdprsubjectaccessrequest.co.uk**.

Whilst reading this book, if you find there is a particular setting on your device that you need help with, or a subject you would like to take a deeper dive in to, then take a look on my Real or Catfish website as it is full of useful advice - it also has a section relating to this book, which includes some useful "How To" videos.

It is important to remember that **cybercriminals, and technologies, are constantly changing and adapting,** and because of that your skills and awareness will need to adapt over time too.

I hope you enjoy the book and that it is of great help to you...

CHAPTER TWO

The Digital Wild West - Understanding the Landscape of Online Threats

"Welcome to the internet - the most powerful tool ever created by humans… but also one of the most dangerous places to let your guard down."

Every day, billions of people connect to the internet. We bank, shop, chat, date, work, and play online. But while you're checking your email or scrolling through social media, someone, somewhere, is trying to scam you.

The internet has become a "digital Wild West" - full of opportunity, but also lawless in places, where cybercriminals and unsavoury characters roam and prey on the unsuspecting. This chapter is an introduction to, and your map of, that landscape: what dangers are out there, how they work, and why average people, not just corporations or governments, are targeted every day.

Toby or not Toby? That is the Question

Why You're a Target

You don't have to be rich, famous, or a tech genius to become a victim of online crime. In fact, being 'somewhat average' makes you an ideal target.

What makes the average person a target?
- You use online banking, email, and social media.
- You probably have a smartphone as well as a computer or tablet.
- You may not realise how much of your personal info is available online.
- And most importantly: You are human, which means you can be tricked, rushed, frightened, or flattered - the exact buttons scammers know how to push.

Cybercriminals have learned that they don't need to hack the complex firewalls and servers of large corporations or governments to profit, they just need to trick enough regular people into clicking a malicious link or giving up a little too much personal information.

A Global Anti-Scam Alliance report shows the total financial cost of cyber scams worldwide soared to a shocking $1.03 trillion in 2024 - that figure is so large that it is bigger than the entire GDP of Switzerland.

The Big Picture: Common Online Threats
Here's a breakdown of the key dangers that we will explore throughout this book. You can think of these as the "most wanted" in our digital Wild West:

1. Phishing
Emails or texts that pretend to be from a trusted entity, like your bank or Amazon for example, trying to get you to click a link and enter your login credentials.

2. Romance Scams & Sextortion
Fraudsters who create fake identities, forming online relationships to manipulate victims both emotionally and financially.

3. Malware and Viruses
Malicious software that can infect your device, steal your files, monitor what you do and what you type, malware can even lock your files and photos and hold it to ransom.

4. Financial Fraud
Fake job offers, bogus investment opportunities, or scams involving money transfers, crypto investment opportunities and even gift cards.

5. Identity Theft
Criminals stealing your personal information to open bank

accounts, take out loans, or impersonate you.

6. Social Engineering
Manipulation tactics that trick you into giving away personal information, passwords or allowing the criminals access to your accounts - often without you realising it.

7. Fake Websites & Online Stores
Convincing replicas of real websites designed to steal your info or money.

The Tools of the Trade: What Scammers Use
Cybercriminals aren't just sitting at keyboards anymore. They use sophisticated tools and techniques that evolve constantly, and with the recent growth in popularity of Artificial Intelligence (AI) it is becoming increasingly harder to detect.

Here are a few examples:
- **Spoofed Emails & Caller IDs:** Make it *look* like a message or call is from your bank, employer or a relative.
- **Malicious Links:** Delivered in fake emails, on social media, or even by text message.
- **Social Media Profiling:** Scammers use what you post publicly to make their attacks more convincing.
- **Deepfakes & AI-generated content:** Increasingly used to impersonate voices or faces in pictures, video or audio.

A Typical Example: The 'Grandma PayPal Scam'
Let's say you're a grandmother who gets an email from "PayPal" saying your account has been charged £700. You have no idea what that transaction is, but the email contains a

link and a warning: "If you don't recognise this transaction then act fast to cancel the payment".

You click the link, log in, and enter some personal info. But the website wasn't real - instead, it was a phishing page. Now, the scammer has your PayPal login details, your home address, and possibly even your credit card information. They go on a spending spree using your PayPal account.

This isn't hypothetical - this happens thousands of times every single day.

But I Have Antivirus - Isn't That Enough?
Good question. Antivirus software is helpful, but **it's only one piece of the puzzle**. Most online scams target your **mind**, not your machine.

Think of antivirus like a seatbelt in your car - it is vital, but it doesn't stop reckless drivers. You still need to stay alert, make smart decisions, and avoid dangerous roads.

That's why **this book focuses on education and habits**, not just tools. Because the number 1 way to protect yourself online is to understand how these scams work and how to recognise them.

Understanding the Criminal Mindset
Cybercriminals are very much like con artists - they are clever, patient, and always testing new angles. Here's what drives them:

- **Profit:** Most cybercrime is financially motivated.
- **Anonymity:** The Internet makes it easy for them to hide their true identity.

- **Scalability:** One scam can target thousands of people in just a few minutes.
- **Psychology:** They don't need to break in - they convince you to open the door.

Unlike traditional criminals, online scammers don't need to be in the same country, or even the same continent, to reach you.

How Much Is Cybercrime Really Costing Us?

Here are a few sobering cybercrime statistics that I have pulled together from various sources:

- In 2024, losses globally to all types of cybercrime were estimated at £7 trillion.
- The average romance scam victim loses more than £8,000.
- A high percentage of phishing attacks are aimed at individuals, not businesses.

And the numbers are rising every year.

Who's Most at Risk?

Whilst anyone can be targeted, some groups are hit more frequently:

Older Adults - Less tech-savvy; the more trusting of us

Teens & Young Adults - They overshare online and can use risky apps

Remote Workers - Use home networks and may not follow their employers security policies

Small Business Owners - Often have limited IT resources but can offer a high payoff for criminals

Key Concepts You'll Learn in This Book

Here's a quick preview of what we'll cover in upcoming chapters - in no particular order:

- How to spot a scam before it tricks you
- What to do if you think you've been compromised
- How to protect your accounts, data, and identity
- How scammers manipulate emotions - and how to resist manipulation
- Which tools and habits make you significantly safer

Glossary

Some basic cybersecurity terms to become familiar with:

Phishing - Fake communication designed to trick you into giving up personal info

Malware - Malicious software (e.g. viruses, spyware, ransomware)

Two Factor Authentication (2FA) - A second layer of security, like a code sent to your phone

VPN - A service that encrypts your Internet traffic and helps hides your location

Social Engineering - Tricking people into revealing confidential information

Don't worry if some of this is new to you, I'll unpack all of it step-by-step.

Key Takeaways:

Let's wrap this chapter up with a few actionable pieces of advice right away:

✓ **If something feels urgent or threatening online, pause**

and verify. Scammers thrive on urgency and panic.

✓ **Never share personal information through links in texts or emails** - instead, go directly to the official website by typing the URL in to your browser.

✓ **Treat your online identity like your home** - lock the doors, know who's knocking, and never leave the keys lying around.

✓ **Stay curious.** If you're unsure about something, take the time to search for more information online or ask a trusted friend.

Summary: A Map Through the Digital Frontier

The digital world isn't going away, and neither are the threats. But knowledge is your best defence.

In this book, you'll learn not only **what** the dangers are, but **how to spot and stop them**, using the same awareness and common sense you'd use in the real world.

Stay alert. Stay sceptical. And stay with me, you're about to get much harder to scam.

CHAPTER THREE

The Psychology of Online Scams - How Criminals Manipulate Trust

"Online scams don't just trick your computer. They trick your brain."

Hackers and scammers don't always need advanced technology to steal your data or your money. Often, they rely on **human psychology** - the same tricks that con artists, magicians and manipulators have used for centuries. The digital age just gives them a faster, wider stage.

In this chapter, you'll learn:
- The psychological principles behind scams
- Why smart people fall for online fraud
- Common emotional triggers exploited by scammers
- How "social engineering" works in real attacks
- Mental models for staying calm and cautious online

Why Understanding Psychology Matters
Cybersecurity isn't just about firewalls, anti-viruses, and strong passwords - it's about how **you think, react, and decide** in digital environments.

Online scammers:
- Bypass security systems and software by targeting **you**, the human
- Exploit **emotion over logic**
- Use high-pressure tactics and **urgency**
- Manipulate trust using fake authority or affection

A Real Life Example:
I have a client whose business banking account was accessed by a scammer - using basic psychology they convinced my client's mobile phone provider to carry out a SIM swap - they took over my client's phone number and were able to receive the 2FA passcodes his bank sent when logging in.

How did they do it? They had already phished the bank account details from an employee at my client's company, the scammer then called the mobile phone provider and spun a story about being in hospital after a serious car crash (they used urgency and emotion). For some unknown reason, the mobile phone provider believed the story and initiated a SIM swap - giving the scammer my client's mobile phone number.

Pro Tip: Later in this book I discuss why an Authenticator app is more secure than using SMS for 2FA - an Authenticator app isn't affected by a SIM swap scam.

Knowing the psychological tricks gives you power. It lets you spot the trap **before** it's sprung.

The 7 Principles of Scam Psychology

These principles are based on foundational concepts in persuasion and behavioural science - some of you may recognise the work of Dr. Robert Cialdini:

1. Authority - *"I'm calling from your bank."*

People tend to obey figures of authority - people in uniforms, job titles or official-sounding language.

Real-life example:

A scammer pretending to be "Microsoft Support" gains remote access to a user's PC because they speak confidently and use technical jargon the user doesn't understand.

Defence:

Be sceptical of anyone who claims to be "from IT", "your bank" or "from the government" unless you are the one who initiated the contact. Always verify they are who they say they are - which is most easily achieved by looking up the correct business phone number online and calling them back.

2. Urgency & Fear - *"Act now or you'll lose everything!"*

Scammers create panic to shut down your reasoning. They push you to act before thinking. Your brain in fear mode bypasses logic and goes straight to survival instincts.

Real-life example:
A pop-up in your web browser says your device is infected and urges you to "click here to fix it immediately."

Defence:
Slow down - legitimate companies don't demand instant action through unverified channels. Close the website - better still, quit your web browser and run an anti-virus scan - just in case.

3. Scarcity - *"Only 3 spots left!"*
People have fear of missing out (FOMO). Scarcity increases perceived value - whether it's a fantastic deal, a great job prospect or a romantic interest.

Real-life example:
"Bitcoin investment" scams pressure users with time-sensitive offers that will vanish if the user doesn't act within the next few minutes.

Defence:
If something is real and valuable, it'll still be there tomorrow.

4. Liking - *"You seem cool. Want to chat?"*
We are more likely to trust people that we like. Scammers will build rapport to bypass your suspicion.

Real-life example:
Romance scammers use compliments, shared interests, and

emotional vulnerability to build trust before asking for money.

Defence:
Be cautious when online interactions move quickly from casual to emotional. Real relationships take time.

5. Consistency - *"Didn't you say you trusted me?"*
Once we commit to something - even a small yes - we're more likely to follow through, even against our better judgment.

Real-life example:
Phishing emails that ask users to "just click to confirm" start small, then escalate to bigger asks (like getting you to download malware).

Defence:
Treat every request like a fresh one. Re-evaluate each step critically. Trust Nobody.

6. Reciprocity - *"I did this for you - now help me."*
People feel obligated to return favours. Scammers may offer help, discounts, or gifts to get you to comply.

Real-life example:
Tech support scams that "fix" your computer and then ask for a donation or fee, or the scammer's favourite, iTunes (App Store) gift-cards.

Defence:
Real help doesn't come with pressure. Always decline help that you didn't ask for.

7. Social Proof - *"Thousands of people already signed up!"*
We take cues from others when we're unsure. Fake testimonials and "excellent" reviews, or referrals from "verified users" are all used to make a scam seem credible.

Real-life example:
Fake e-commerce websites with fake reviews and a numerical display counting up, indicating their popularity (albeit fake popularity).

Defence:
Verify reviews on independent platforms. Don't assume popularity equals legitimacy.

Social Engineering in Action
"Social engineering" refers to the use of deception to manipulate people into revealing confidential information.

Common tactics:
These 5 techniques are most commonly used in social engineering attacks:

Phishing - Emails trick you into clicking links or entering passwords

Pretexting - Scammer invents a scenario to get your trust (e.g., "The Payroll Dept. needs your bank details")

Baiting - Offering a fake reward to get you to take an action

Tailgating - Physically following someone into a secure space (in real-world settings)

Quid pro quo - Offering "support" or "recovery" in exchange for harvesting your credentials

A Recent Example (A Well Known Retail Chain):
Using details reported in the press, we can see what happened in this recent, very high-profile case - an attacker posing as a member of staff called the company's IT help desk, pretending they needed to reset their password. The help desk, in wanting to assist, believed them and went ahead with the password reset - giving the attacker access to company systems.

The attacker then unleashed a huge cyberattack across the company, using ransomware - locking the company's data and holding it to ransom. The attack had wide-reaching effect and seriously impacted the company's business for several months.

Why Smart People Fall for Scams
It's not about intelligence - it's about emotion, timing, and manipulation.

Scammers succeed because:
- They catch people when distracted or stressed
- They exploit trust, fear, loneliness, or greed
- They use written **scripts** which have been tested on thousands of people
- They don't need to fool everyone - just enough people

Remember, everyone can be vulnerable under the right circumstances.

How to Outsmart Psychological Manipulation
Try to get used to setting yourself some ground rules that will help you stop and think about the situation - personally I

find rule number 2 the hardest to stick to, and rule number 4 the easiest.

1. Create yourself some "cool-down" rules
Never act on a message (email, text, pop-up) until you've:
- Waited 10 minutes
- Verified the sender's identity
- Thought about whether it benefits *them* more than *you*

2. Label your emotions
If you feel fear, urgency, excitement, or panic - label it.
"This is urgency - and that's a manipulation tactic."
Naming it helps you regain logical control.

3. Think of, and use verification routines
Always confirm major requests through a second channel:
- Don't reply to the email - call the person directly on their published number
- Don't trust the link - type the known URL in to your web browser instead

4. Use "Assume It's a Scam" as your default thought process
Then look for proof that it's **not** a scam - rather than assuming it's legitimate and then afterwards, regrettably, looking for signs of a scam.

Summary
Scammers exploit your mind, not just your machine. By understanding the psychology behind fraud, you can interrupt their playbook and keep control of your decisions.

The goal isn't to be perfect, it's to **be harder to fool than the average person**.

Key Takeaways:
- Online scams rely on emotion, rather than logic
- The 7 principles (authority, urgency, scarcity, etc.) are common across many types of fraud
- Everyone is vulnerable sometimes, which is why habits and a checklist help
- Building emotional awareness helps you stay calm and secure
- When in doubt, assume it's a scam - and then try to verify everything

Security is no longer just a technical issue. It's a human one.

CHAPTER FOUR

Phishing for Trouble - How Scammers Steal Your Information

"They didn't break in, you accidentally opened the door."

Imagine receiving an email from your bank saying your account is locked. There's a link - you click it. The website looks just like your bank's, so you log in to "fix" the issue. But it wasn't real. You just gave your username and password to a scammer.

This is phishing - and it's one of the most common and effective forms of cybercrime today. It is much easier for the criminal to phish for people's credentials than it is for them to try and hack a computer or a business network.

In this chapter, we'll dive into how phishing works, what it looks like, and how to stop it from catching you out.

What Is Phishing?
  Phishing is a cybercrime where attackers impersonate trusted entities - like banks, tech companies, coworkers, or even friends - to trick you into revealing sensitive

information, such as:

- Passwords and login credentials
- Credit and debit card numbers
- Banking information
- National Insurance / Social Security numbers

The name comes from "fishing," as in throwing out bait on a hook and hoping someone bites. The "bait" is the fake email or message, and the "hook" is whatever gets you to act - usually fear, urgency, or curiosity.

Common Types of Phishing Attacks

Phishing isn't just limited to email - scammers use multiple attack channels:

1. Email Phishing

The classic method. You get an email that appears to be from a legitimate company or person. It often contains:

- A sense of urgency: "We have detected suspicious activity on your account!"
- A suspicious link: "Click here to verify whether it was you or not"
- A spoofed sender address: It looks like it is from a real company but isn't

2. Spear Phishing

This is more targeted. Instead of sending the same email to thousands of people at a time, the scammer personalises the message using details about you (like your name, workplace, or hobbies). It it aimed at you personally - like **fishing with a spear** rather than a net.

3. Smishing (SMS Phishing)

A fake message sent by text (SMS) message to your phone, often claiming to be your bank, a delivery service, or even a government agency.

Example: *"Your package has postage owing. Click here to pay the balance."*

4. Vishing (Voice Phishing)

A phone call from someone pretending to be from a trusted company. They may claim there's fraud on your account or ask you to "confirm" your identity and or date of birth.

5. Social Media & Messaging Apps

Phishing links can come through Facebook Messenger, Instagram direct messages (DM's), WhatsApp, Telegram and more - especially if one of your friends' accounts has been compromised and the scammer is using that account to contact you.

Anatomy of a Phishing Message

This section breaks down what a phishing email might look like. Beware though, some phishing emails are extremely well crafted and can look quite believable.

Subject: *"Your Netfix Account Has Been Suspended"*
From: *support@netf1x-secure.com*
Dear Customer,

We were unable to process your payment. Your account will be suspended within 24 hours.

Please update your payment method immediately by clicking the link below:

[Fake Link To Update Billing Info]

Thank you for being a valued customer.

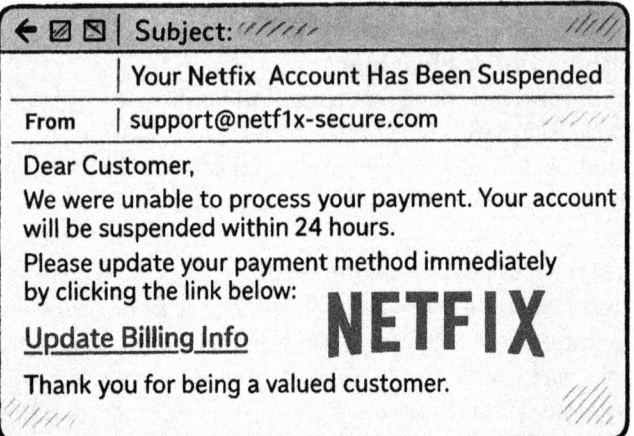

✗ Red Flags:
- The sender's email address is incorrect, the domain shows: netf1x-secure.com
- The message creates a false sense of urgency
- There's a suspicious link in the message (remember to hover over links)
- It's addressed to "Dear Customer" - rather than to your name

These can be subtle, but once you learn to spot them, they stand out like neon signs.

Why Does Phishing Work So Well?
Phishing doesn't rely on cracking passwords or hacking

networks - both of which are actually much harder to do in real life than you would think from watching Hollywood movies. Instead, phishing relies on **psychology**.

Scammers exploit emotions to cloud your judgment:
- **Fear** - "Your account is at risk!"
- **Curiosity** - "See what your friend said about you..."
- **Greed** - "You've won a free iPhone!"
- **Trust** - "This is your boss. I need a quick favour."

Even tech-savvy people fall for phishing when they're tired, distracted, or in a rush.

How Phishers Create Their Traps

Here's what goes into creating a typical phishing attack:

Spoofed Email Address or Website The domain name is often spelled just one letter off, such as paypa1.com instead of paypal.com and other times, it can be completely different.

Brand Imitation Use of the same logos, colours, and layout as the real brand - because the scammer has copied those elements from the real website.

Fake Login Pages It looks legit, but the domain name isn't quite right, or some of the links on the page don't work - if you enter your password on one of these sites, the scammer grabs it instantly

Redirects & Hidden URLs The link might look like it is to apple.com but instead goes to a malicious site when clicked - hover your cursor over the link to see where it really goes. Think of the words you can see as being "decorative text" and the actual URL is hidden from sight, only being revealed when you hover your mouse cursor over it.

Malicious Attachments Clicking these can install malware on your device. Never open any attachments that you weren't expecting, especially when you don't know the sender.

Real-World Example: The Boss Email Scam
A receptionist at a small company receives an urgent email from the CEO:

"Can you send me the company credit card info for an emergency purchase?"

The email address looked legit and the tone felt right. She sent the details - only later did she realise it wasn't really the CEO - just a carefully crafted, spoofed email.

This kind of **business email compromise (BEC)** causes billions in losses annually - and it starts with a simple phishing attack.

Another example of **BEC** is when a scammer has gained access to an employee's email account - by phishing their login credentials - the scammer then looks for any invoices the employee has sent and changes the bank details on the invoices to his own bank details - the scammer then uses the compromised email account to re-send the invoices to unsuspecting customers. The customer pays the invoice using the new bank details - straight in to the scammer's pocket. This is commonly known as ***Business Invoice Fraud.***

Pro Tip: If you receive an email from a company notifying you of a change in their bank details, **phone the company using their published number (not the number given in the**

email) and confirm if the change is genuine or not.

How to Spot Phishing Like a Pro

Here's a quick phishing detection checklist:

✓ Check the sender's email address. Even just one wrong letter is a red flag.

✓ Hover your cursor over links. If the URL looks shady, don't click it.

✓ Check spelling and grammar. Many phishing emails have subtle mistakes.

✓ Never share sensitive info over email. Legitimate companies won't ask for it.

✓ Look for generic greetings. "Dear Customer" instead of your name.

✓ Beware of urgent language. Pressure to act fast is a classic tactic.

What to Do if You Suspect Phishing

These tips are important to remember, as any action you take on a phishing email can signal to the scammer that your email address is active and therefore still a prime target - and you don't want that.

- Don't click anything. Not even the unsubscribe link as it could be a trap.
- Don't reply. It tells the scammer your email account is still active.
- Report it - Most email providers let you mark emails as phishing or junk.
- If it's mimicking a company (like PayPal), report it to them directly.
- Warn others. Especially coworkers or family

members who may be targeted too.

Tools That Help Against Phishing

Technology can help, but don't rely on it alone. Some helpful tools include:

- **Spam filters:** Most email platforms block known scams.
- **Browser alerts:** Browsers can warn you before visiting fake websites.
- **Password managers:** If using autofill, it will only work on legitimate sites.
- **2FA (Two-Factor Authentication):** Protects your accounts even if someone gets your password.
- **Disable the loading of remote images** in your email settings.

We'll talk more about tools and security again in a later chapter.

Phishing by the Numbers

These are some recent phishing figures that I have seen mentioned online over recent months:

- Over 3.4 billion phishing emails are sent daily.
- The vast majority of data breaches start with a phishing email.
- 82% of people admit they've clicked on a phishing link at least once.
- The average loss per phishing attack is £100, in 2021 this amounted to a total in the region of £33 million

"Phish or Legit?" Quiz

You receive an email from Amazon that says:

"Unusual activity detected on your account. Log in to verify recent purchases."

It includes a link to what looks like the Amazon login page.

What should you do?
A) Click the link and log in to check your orders
B) In your browser go to amazon.co.uk - type it in manually
C) Reply to the email and ask for confirmation

Answer: B. Always go directly to the site yourself to check - never click on suspicious links.

Summary

Phishing is simple, cheap, and alarmingly effective, which is why it remains one of the top cyber threats today.

Anything that has a perceived value can be the target of phishing - even store loyalty cards.

But once you know what to look for, phishing becomes easy to spot. The key is slowing down, verifying the sender, and never acting purely on emotion.

If something seems too urgent or too good to be true - it probably is

CHAPTER FIVE

Love Gone Wrong - Romance Scams and Emotional Exploitation

"It wasn't just my heart they stole - it was also my savings and my pride."

Online dating has changed the way we connect. But as much as it's created opportunities for love, it's also opened the door for a dark kind of predator: the romance scammer.

They don't use malware or brute-force hacking tools. Their weapon is emotion, trust, vulnerability, and loneliness. Romance scams cost victims billions every year and unlike phishing, these scams can take months to unfold.

In this chapter, we'll explore:
- How romance scams work
- Who gets targeted (it's not just who you think)
- The psychology behind the scam
- Warning signs and how to protect yourself or your loved ones

What Is a Romance Scam?

A **romance scam** occurs when a scammer builds an emotional, and often romantic, relationship with a "target" online, with the goal of manipulating them into sending money, sharing personal information, or doing things they normally wouldn't do.

It often begins innocently:
- A connection or message on a dating site or social media
- A flattering compliment
- A compelling backstory
- A random message on WhatsApp that appears to be a wrong number

But it ends in financial loss, betrayal, and, frequently, deep emotional trauma.

The Psychology of the Scam

Romance scammers play the **long game**. They don't immediately ask for money. They build trust first, they listen, they flatter and they mirror your values. The relationship often escalates quickly into expressions of love, making plans for the future and includes contact on a daily basis.

Why it works:
- **Loneliness:** Especially after a divorce, widowhood, or social isolation
- **Desire for connection:** People want to be seen and valued
- **Social engineering:** Scammers study their victims and say exactly what they want to hear - they sometimes even pretend to be their victim's favourite celebrity.
- **Shame resistance:** Victims may ignore red flags and

avoid admitting they were fooled, because they are embarrassed or ashamed to have been caught out. Some people have been known to "accept the lie" rather than end the attention they are receiving - even though they know it's a scam.

The scammers make you feel special, and they weaponise that feeling against you.

How the Scam Unfolds

A fairly typical romance scam may proceed like this, step-by-step:

1. Initial Contact

• Through dating apps, social media, random WhatsApp messages and common interest groups online.

• Conversation often starts with flattery or a compliment.

2. Emotional Connection

• Frequent messages, long conversations and terms of endearment.

• "I've never felt this way before" or "I think you're the one."

3. Isolation

• They discourage you from talking to friends or family about them.

• They claim "others won't understand what we have."

4. Introduction of a Crisis

• An Emergency: "I need money to fly to see you" or "My child needs surgery" or "I need to buy clothes for a work event"

• Scammers often ask for:

- Bank transfers or Wire transfers
- Gift cards - especially "App Store & iTunes" gift cards
- Cryptocurrency - usually in Bitcoin
- Your bank account or credit card details

5. More Excuses
- If you pay, then soon another "crisis" arises.
- Their trip is delayed, or their travel visa was denied.
- The hospital needs more money.

6. Silence or Disappearance
- When the scammer feels you won't pay anymore, they disappear.
- Or worse - they continue to manipulate you for months.

When you run out of money the scammer may encourage you to **submit a false insurance claim** in order to extract even more money from you, as "It doesn't hurt anybody". But if you do this you have just committed insurance fraud - **the scammer doesn't care**.

Victims Lists:

Do you know that scammers have **'Victims Lists'** which they share with other scammers? If you have sent a scammer money, or your ID documents or you seem an easy target, your details will probably be added to one of these lists - and for years to come, you will be targeted by **all sorts of investment scams** and **fake 'money recovery' companies**.

Don't let yourself be taken in by fake businesses claiming to be able to recover the crypto you lost to a scammer, only law enforcement agencies, such as your local police, can request this type of information from crypto exchanges in order to identify the owner of crypto wallets used in the scam.

Unfortunately, **the odds of being able to recover any crypto currency** sent to a scammer **are so slim that it may as well be zero**. Any company contacting you offering to recover it for you is, I'm afraid, just another scam (because you are on a **Victims List**).

A Popular Type of Romance Scam

Your "romantic interest" tells you about the fantastic investment opportunity that they have just made a fortune investing in. You ask if you can get in on this scheme too. They, of course, say yes and **you send them your money,** usually **in crypto currency** such as Bitcoin.

Many of these crypto investment scams have a very believable-looking website or app which will show you your money growing in your investment account - but it's fake.

The app or website has been carefully crafted as part of the scam. The scammer may even put some "additional crypto of their own" in to your account to help you along a bit. Of course, the scammer hasn't actually put additional crypto in to your account - rather, the fake app or website is just **displaying numbers that the scammer has typed in to it** - your money isn't in there either, it has gone elsewhere.

When the time comes that you want to withdraw your funds, **suddenly there are some previously unmentioned taxes or fees to pay** - so begrudgingly, you pay those fees - but then, out of nowhere, there is **"trouble verifying your identity"** and **your "account gets frozen" permanently**. And that's the last you will see of your money I'm afraid. It's all a very well crafted scam.

This is an image of an app that scammers were using in one of the cases I investigated a few years ago - fully functional and very believable.

This type of romance investment fraud is currently known as a **"Pig Butchering Scam"**.

If you want to see the size of some of these operations, then **I suggest watching Jim Browning's "Inside a Pig Butchering Scam"** video on YouTube. It exposes the scale of one of these operations. This particular operation even **has a female model on staff** to make face-to-face video calls with their male victims. I'll put a link to it on my Real or Catfish site.

Pro Tip: *A request for any kind of money is always a serious red flag* - especially if you've never met them in person. Trust your gut - don't make excuses for them.

Where Romance Scammers Lurk

Scammers don't just use dating sites. They use every platform where people connect:

- **Dating apps** - stolen photos, overseas work, military, nurse, etc

- **Social media** - looks like a model, may be a cloned account of a celebrity or a celeb's "secret second account"

- **Messaging apps** - attractive picture, sends a random Hello message, which is a "wrong number"

- **Niche communities** - Gaming forums, religious groups, support groups and Discord

Even the business platform, **LinkedIn**, in some cases.

A Typical Romance Scam Profile

Most scammers use fake profiles (aka "catfishing") and pretend to be someone who seems attractive, impressive, and emotionally available.

Common personas include:
- A soldier deployed overseas or someone working overseas
- A doctor with a charity or organisation based overseas
- An oil rig worker
- A successful entrepreneur
- A single parent widowed in tragic circumstances

Why these personas? Because:
- They sound respectable
- They explain why they can't meet in person

- They provide cover for time zone differences or delays

The Financial & Emotional Toll

Romance scams cost victims around the world more than **£970 million annually** (2024), over **£92 million of that figure was from victims in the UK**. But that's just what's reported - many victims never come forward out of shame, guilt, or fear of judgment.

Typical financial losses can range from **a few hundred pounds to well over £200,000.**

But the emotional damage can be worse:
- Loss of trust in people
- Depression, anxiety, PTSD
- Broken families and friendships

Who Gets Targeted?

Anyone can be a victim, but scammers tend to focus on these groups:

Often lonely, financially secure, less tech-savvy

Emotionally vulnerable

Fewer social interactions

Scammers often pose as younger men

Scammers often pose as attractive young women

Top 10 Warning Signs of a Romance Scam

There are many red flags that you can look for, but by far these are the most common warning signs:

They:

✗ Claim to be overseas or in a remote job (military, oil rig, charity, etc)
✗ Profess love unusually quickly
✗ Avoid video calls or face-to-face meetings
✗ Eventually talk of money - a "great investment" or even "just to borrow"
✗ Always have a story: stolen passport, sick relative, lost job, etc
✗ Keep making excuses not to meet
✗ Ask for help transferring packages, money, or crypto currency
✗ Try to isolate you from any friends and family who are suspicious
✗ Profile photos are generic or reverse-searchable online
✗ Move communication off the dating platform quickly, on to messaging apps.

Why do scammers want to **quickly move the conversation away from the dating app** and on to a messaging app or texts? Because the **dating apps monitor messages sent in chat** for key words, phrases and typical signs of a scammer. The scammer needs to take your conversation elsewhere before they get exposed and have their account frozen.

How to Protect Yourself (and Others)

✓ 1. Verify Their Identity
- Use reverse image search (Yandex, TinEye or PimEyes) to see if their photos appear elsewhere. (See the later chapter on how to do this)
- Ask specific questions about local news or daily life in their location.

✓ 2. Be Sceptical of Long-Distance Romance

- If they refuse to video chat or visit after months - something's wrong.
- Ask yourself: *"If this was happening to my friend, would it sound suspicious?"*

✓ 3. Never Send Money to Someone You Haven't Met
- Not for plane tickets, medical bills, crypto, or any reason.
- Don't share banking info, passport scans, photos of your driving licence, etc.

✓ 4. Talk to a Trusted Friend or Family Member
- Scammers want to isolate you from family and friends.
- Others may see the red flags that you don't.

✓ 5. Report the Profile
- To the platform you initially met them through
- To your country's fraud agency e.g. Action Fraud (UK) and the FTC (US)

Don't Be A Money Mule

Because they are always looking for ways to exploit their victims, some romance **scammers might ask you to help them** out because of **a banking problem**, or other lie, such as **receiving money from "their friend"** who owes it to them. You want to help, so you receive the funds in to your bank and then you send that money on, either as crypto currency or as a regular bank transfer.

You said yes because you trust them - except **you have just unwittingly committed a crime - money laundering.** And you may well find yourself being arrested and ending up in court.

Elderly and Vulnerable Victims
Romance scams often target:
- Seniors
- Divorced or widowed individuals
- Those living alone

Scammers may spend **months** grooming victims. If you suspect someone you love is being scammed:
- Be compassionate - don't shame or accuse them
- Ask neutral questions: "Have you video chatted with them?" or "Have you sent money?"
- Help them look up the person's photos using reverse image tools
- Involve a trusted third-party or a professional if needed

Real-World Examples

Example 1: The Crypto Romance Scam
In 2022, a woman in California lost over **$1.2 million** to a man she met on a dating app who introduced her to cryptocurrency "investments." He showed fake profits on a cloned trading site. She wired money in increasing amounts until she realised she couldn't withdraw any of the funds.

Example 2: The Facebook Soldier
An elderly man in the UK met a "U.S. Army nurse" on social media She convinced him she needed money to return from deployment. He sent over £40,000 before his family intervened.

Example 3: The 'Army Captain'
A 63-year-old woman met "James" online, a charming U.S.

Army captain stationed in Syria. They chatted daily for months. He said he wanted to marry her when he returned.

But he was "having trouble accessing his funds" and asked her to help pay for leave paperwork. Over a six month period, she wired him $45,000 - her retirement savings. It was all fake. His photos were stolen from a real soldier. The scammer vanished.

Tools and Resources

You may find these additional online resources helpful in identifying and reporting romance scammers:

- **Yandex, Google, PimEyes, etc** - Reverse Image Search to check if profile pictures are stolen (see chapter 15 for more information)
- **realorcatfish.com** - my website with free resources, videos and detailed help
- **cobalt-ict.com** - my company website - for when you need advanced help, or have been scammed out of a significant amount of money.
- **actionfraud.org.uk** - Report scams in the UK
- **reportfraud.ftc.gov** - Report scams in the US
- **scamwatch.gov.au** - Report scams in Australia

"But What If They're Real?"

This is the hardest part - **anyone can fall for romance scams** - and once drawn in to the scammer's web of deception it can be very hard for people to accept that their online love interest is actually a scammer. If you are trying to help a loved one, you may find that they initially get angry or frustrated with you for questioning things - be prepared to stick with it and help them to understand, try not to throw your arms up in the air and walk away.

Ask yourself:
- Have I ever seen this person on a live video call?
- Have I verified their name, photos, or backstory?
- Would a real person ask this of someone they've never met?
- It is quite common for a victim to not want to hear the truth

If the answer feels off - that's because it probably is.

Summary

Romance scams aren't about gullibility. They're about **manipulation, vulnerability, and trust.** These scams work because humans are wired to seek a connection.

But you don't have to be paranoid - just cautious.

Love online is possible - but so is deception.

Trust slowly. Verify everything and protect your heart, and your wallet.

CHAPTER SIX

The Scammer's Playbook - Social Engineering Tactics That Trick Even the Smartest People

"They didn't hack my computer, they hacked my trust."

You might imagine cybercriminals hunched over laptops, breaking through firewall security and cracking passwords with brute-force programs. But the truth is, most successful cyberattacks don't need advanced hacking tools - just a little psychology.

The weapon? **Social engineering** - the art of manipulating people into giving up information, access, or money.

In this chapter, you'll learn:
- What social engineering is
- The most common tactics (with some real examples)
- Why they work so well
- How to spot and stop them before it's too late

What Is Social Engineering?
Social engineering is a form of **psychological manipulation** used to trick people into revealing confidential

information or performing actions that compromise security. It relies on human emotions rather than technology.

You can think of it like a con artist using their charm to trick you into handing over your keys. Except in this case, the "keys" are your passwords, financial details, or the control of your online accounts.

Common Social Engineering Tactics
Let's explore the most widely used and dangerous techniques in a scammer's toolkit:

1. Phishing
What it is: As we have already discussed, phishing involves fake emails, messages, or websites that look real - designed to steal your login credentials or install malware.

Example:
An email claims to be from your bank:
"Suspicious activity detected. Please log in immediately to verify your account."

The link leads to a convincing but fake website. You enter your password… and it goes straight to the scammer.

Variants:
- **Spear phishing** - Targeted to a specific person (e.g. a company accountant)
- **Whaling** - Targeting high-level executives
- **Smishing** - Phishing via SMS text message
- **Vishing** - Voice phishing via phone calls

2. Pretexting
What it is: The attacker creates a fake identity or scenario

to build trust and trick the victim into revealing information.

Example:
A scammer calls pretending to be from IT support:
"Hi, we're updating the password policy. Can I confirm your old login before we reset it?"

They sound official, use industry jargon, and may even spoof the company's phone number.

3. Baiting
What it is: Offering something tempting (like a free app to download or a free USB drive) to trick the victim into running malware.

Example:
You find a USB stick labeled "Executive Salaries 2025" on the ground in the office parking lot. Curiosity wins and you plug it in to your computer. The malware activates...

It's not fiction - companies have fallen victim to this exact tactic.

4. Quid Pro Quo
What it is: Offering a service or benefit in exchange for information.

Example:
A caller offers to help fix a printer issue - but asks for your network login first. You think it's helpful support. In reality, it's a scammer harvesting credentials.

5. Impersonation
What it is: Pretending to be someone you trust - a

coworker, IT admin, CEO, or even a family member.

Example:
You get a text from your "boss" while they're supposedly travelling:

"Hey, can you urgently buy some gift cards for a client event? I'll reimburse you later."

You activate the gift card - the phone number was spoofed, and the gift card balance codes go straight to a scammer's account.

Why These Tactics Work

Social engineering attacks succeed because they exploit **basic human instincts**, let's examine some of the psychological triggers:

Urgency - "Act now or your account will be closed!"

Authority - "This is the CEO. I need this wire transfer done ASAP."

Trust - "I'm from tech support. I need you to install an app so I can control your computer to fix the issue."

Curiosity - "Click here to see who viewed your profile!"

Greed - "You've won a free iPhone!"

Fear - "Your account has been hacked. Click to secure it now."

These tactics aren't new - con artists have used them for centuries. But in the digital world, they scale much faster and can be automated.

A literal "Playbook for Scammers"

The two pages in the image above are taken from a Chinese language guide-book (a script) that the scam operators working in organised crime gangs use. It includes day-by-day, week-by-week instructions on how the scam operator should build the relationship with, and then scam, their victims.

Real-World Examples

Example 1: The Google Docs Phish

In 2017, a phishing campaign spread like wildfire. Users received an email saying someone had shared a Google Doc with them.

The link led to a fake Google permission page that, when approved, gave the attacker access to the victim's Gmail account and their files on Google Drive. Thousands were compromised in hours - including journalists and government workers.

Example 2: The Twitter Bitcoin Hack

In 2020, attackers used social engineering to trick Twitter employees into giving up admin credentials. They used this access to take over high-profile accounts (Elon Musk, Bill Gates, Barack Obama, etc) and post:

"Send Bitcoin to this address, and we'll double it!"

Over $100,000 was sent by unsuspecting people before the posts were removed.

Example 3: The Fake CEO

A finance employee at a mid-sized company received an urgent email from the "CEO" (it was actually from a spoofed email address):

"I need you to wire $20,000 to a new vendor immediately. Here are the account details."

The employee complied without question - only to learn the real CEO had never sent the message.

This kind of attack - known as **business email compromise (BEC)** - cost U.S. companies over **$2.4 billion** in 2023 alone.

How to Spot Social Engineering Attacks

You can use this quick **"Think Before You Click"** checklist to help spot the signs of social engineering:

✗ *Unexpected message* - "Your Amazon package is delayed - click here." (But you didn't order anything.)
✗ *Generic greeting* - "Dear customer" instead of your name

✗ *Bad grammar or spelling* - "Pleese verify your bank detail imediately"

✗ *Suspicious links* - Hover your mouse cursor over the link - does it match the sender's domain?

✗ *Strange requests* - Gift cards, urgent wire transfers, login information, etc

✗ *Unusual timing* - An email from "IT" at 3 a.m. asking for credentials

How to Defend Against Social Engineering

Here's how even non-tech-savvy users can protect themselves:

✓ 1. Be Sceptical

If it sounds urgent, threatening, or too good to be true - slow down. Don't click or reply right away.

✓ 2. Verify Requests

Got an odd message from your boss or friend? Call them directly to confirm. Don't rely on the message itself.

✓ 3. Use Two-Factor Authentication (2FA)

Even if someone steals your password, they can't log in without your second factor (such as a code sent to your phone).

✓ 4. Educate Yourself and Others

Scammers evolve. Stay informed. Help friends and family learn about common scams.

✓ 5. Keep Software Updated

Many phishing attacks also try to exploit browser, operating system or app vulnerabilities. Keep everything updated.

✓ 6. Use Spam Filters and Security Tools

Modern email providers like Gmail and Outlook filter out many phishing attempts - but not all. Security extensions like uBlock Origin or browser warnings help too.

✗ 7. Never Allow Someone to Install Remote Access Software

Scammers will offer to help you with transactions and ask you to install remote support software on your computer - never give anyone you don't know access to your computer or accounts.

Quick Tools You Can Use

Of the four tools listed below, I use VirusTotal most frequently - you can paste a website's URL in to VirusTotal and it will scan the site for malware and other issues - for free.

haveibeenpwned.com - Check if your email/passwords were leaked

virustotal.com - Scan suspicious files or URLs

Bitwarden / 1Password - Secure password managers

Your email spam filter - Block phishing attempts easily and automatically

Protecting Friends and Family

Older adults and less tech-savvy people are especially vulnerable.

Here's how to help them:

✓ Sit down and explain common red flags
✓ Help them enable 2FA on email and banking

✓ Show them how to verify links and hover to preview
✓ Encourage them to call you before acting on any suspicious messages

Remind them **"It's always okay to double-check. Scammers want you to rush."**

Summary

Social engineering doesn't require coding skills - just human insight. It's one of the most dangerous and effective tactics in cybercrime because it targets **people**, not systems. But once you understand how it works, you're much harder to fool.

Stay curious. Stay cautious. And if something feels off - it probably is.

CHAPTER SEVEN

Fake Websites, Scams & Spoofs - Spotting Online Deception

"If it looks real, sounds real, and feels real... it might still be fake."

Scammers are no longer just hiding in the dark alleys of the web - they are crafting sleek, convincing websites and online storefronts that can fool anyone. And while the designs may vary, their goals are the same:

- Steal your money
- Collect your personal information
- Infect your device with malware

In this chapter, we'll break down:
- How fake websites and spoofed pages work
- The psychology behind them
- Real examples that have tricked millions
- How to spot fakes like a cybersecurity pro
- Steps to stay safe while browsing and shopping online

Let's start by understanding the playing field.

What Are Fake Websites?

A **fake website** is any site that imitates a real one - or creates a false identity - to deceive visitors.

It might:
- **Pretend to be your bank** or a parcel delivery service
- **Offer luxury goods** at too-good-to-be-true prices
- **Host malicious downloads** disguised as software
- **Mimic login pages** for email, social media, online shopping, etc
- **Trick you** into entering credit card or personal details

Scammers use these types of sites in phishing campaigns, fake ads, social media posts, and even text messages. Many are so convincing that even the most careful of people have fallen for them.

Spoofing vs. Typosquatting vs. Cloning

These terms often overlap, but we can easily clarify the main differences:

Spoofing: A fake version of a legitimate site, often sent via phishing
  Example: login-paypal.com

Typosquatting: Slightly misspelled domain names to catch typing errors
  Example: amaz0n.com, facebok.net

Cloning: A complete copy of a real site's layout and branding
  Example: Visually identical but a slightly different domain name

Why They Work

Scammers rely on many things to manipulate their victims, including:

- **Visual mimicry** - using logos, colours, and layouts that match the real sites
- **Emotion** - urgency, fear or excitement
- **Inattention** - you're busy and click without inspecting URLs
- **Overload** - too many tabs open to notice small details

They know that humans are the weakest link, and they design and act accordingly.

Common Fake Website Scenarios

1. Fake E-commerce Stores
- Offer unbelievable deals (e.g. iPhones for $99)
- Steal your payment info or never ship the product
- Disappear in weeks

✗ **Red flag**: No contact info, reviews or clear return policies

2. Spoofed Login Pages
- Mimic login portals for email, banks or cloud storage
- Captures your credentials as soon as you log in

✗ **Red flag**: URL slightly off (e.g. gmaiI.com with a capital "i" for the L)

3. Fake Antivirus Sites
- Pop-ups warn: "Your computer is infected!"
- Prompt you to install a fake virus scanner (which is actually malware)

✗ **Red flag**: Browser hijacks, loud alarm sounds, countdown timers

4. Charity Scams
- Use crises (e.g. natural disasters or war) to appeal for donations
- Pose as well-known charities with slightly altered names or domains

✗ **Red flag**: Only asks for crypto or gift cards as donation

5. Government or Tax Scams
- Fake tax refund or stimulus payment sites
- Designed to collect Government ID, banking info or download ransomware

✗ **Red flag**: Poor grammar, non .gov or .gov.uk domain

How to Spot a Fake Website
This 5-point inspection checklist will help you to spot a fake site:

✓ 1. Check the URL Carefully
- Does the domain look suspicious?
- secure-paypal-login.com → FAKE
- paypal.com → REAL
- Watch for:
- Misspellings - amaz0n, gooogle etc
- Unusual top-level domains - .co, .net, .biz instead of .com or .co.uk
- Strange subdomains - account-security.paypal.com.fake.net

✓ 2. Look for HTTPS - But Don't Trust It Alone
- A padlock 🔒 in the address bar means your browser session is encrypted, **BUT** it does not necessarily mean the website is legitimate or safe
- HTTPS uses a SSL certificate which is installed on the webserver

- Many **fake sites use SSL certificates (HTTPS)** to appear legitimate

✓ 3. Check the Design and Grammar
- Are there blurry logos? Typos? Poor formatting? Is there a privacy policy?
- Legitimate businesses invest in quality design and comply with regulations

✓ 4. Search for Reviews and Reputation
- Google the site's name along with words like "scam" or "reviews"
- You can also use sites like these to check its reputation:
- ScamAdviser.com
- Trustpilot.com

✓ 5. Verify Contact Info
- No phone number or physical address listed? Very likely a fake site.
- Using a generic Gmail or Yahoo email address can also be a red flag

A few years ago, one SSL certificate authority was reported to have issued over 15,000 certificates for domain names with the word "PayPal" used in them - only PayPal themselves should have a certificate with that in the domain name - it would be reasonable to assume that those 15,000 SSL certificates were for use by scammers to create websites impersonating Paypal.

Pro Tip: "Hover Before You Click"

Train yourself and others to **hover your mouse cursor over links** before clicking them - when you hover your mouse pointer over a link, your browser will then display the actual link destination as text inside a pop-up tooltip. Whether in an email or on a webpage, this simple habit can quickly expose any hidden danger.

Example:
- **Visible**: www.apple.com
- **Actual** (hover shows): www.apple-secure-login.ru

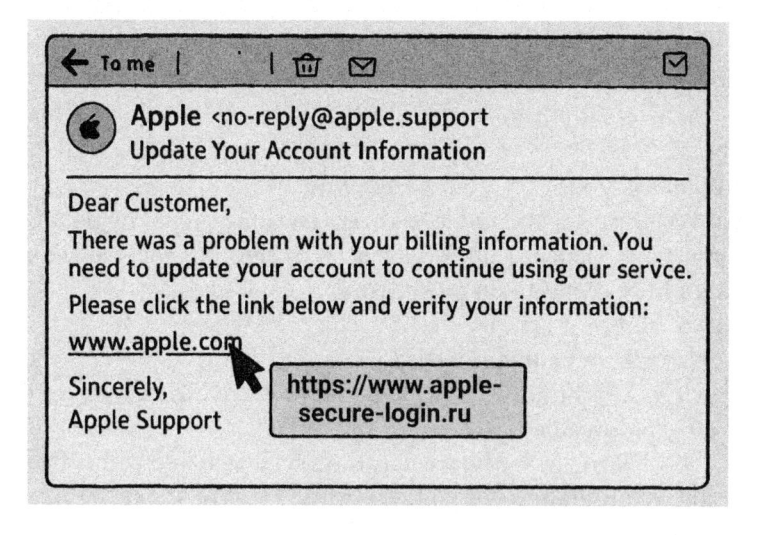

> ← To me
>
> **Apple** <no-reply@apple.support
> Update Your Account Information
>
> Dear Customer,
> There was a problem with your billing information. You need to update your account to continue using our servìce. Please click the link below and verify your information:
> www.apple.com
> Sincerely,   https://www.apple-
> Apple Support secure-login.ru

Think of the displayed text or link as just being decorative - whereas the actual URL activated when you click is 'hidden' by that decorative text and it can be something completely different.

Even small spelling mismatches are a huge red flag - the domain name must be spelled exactly right, there's no such thing a being 'close enough' when it comes to the Internet and email domain names.

Tools to Help You Detect Fakes

Take some time to visit and to learn about these helpful tools. WhoIs lookup will show you when a website domain was created - many scam sites are less than a few months old. And VirusTotal will scan a website and tell you if it will infect your computer with malware or if the website appears to be a phishing site.

www.whois.com/whois/ - Check domain creation date; new sites are riskier

www.virustotal.com/gui/home/url - Scans websites for malware or phishing indicators

What To Do If You Visit a Fake Site

It's always a good idea to carry out some digital hygiene if you have visited a fake website. Carrying out these 6 steps should be sufficient in most cases:

1. **Don't enter any data**
2. **Disconnect from the internet** if you clicked any downloads
3. **Run a malware scan** with a trusted antivirus program
4. **Change any compromised passwords immediately**
5. **Enable two-factor authentication (2FA)** on your account/s
6. **Report the website** at safebrowsing.google.com/safebrowsing/report-url

An Example: The Holiday Deal Trap

During Black Friday, Maria saw a Facebook advert for "Dyson vacuums - 80% off." The website looked professional, and she placed an order.

The site vanished 48 hours later. Her card was charged $300. No vacuum ever arrived.

What happened?
- The site was cloned from Dyson's official site
- It was hosted using a newly registered domain name
- The site ran Facebook ads targeting bargain hunters

If it feels too good to be true, it probably is.

How Scammers Make Sites Look Real

They use multiple techniques to look legitimate, and to trick people, such as:

- **Typosquatting** on slightly misspelled domain names
- **Stolen logos and layouts** copied from the real site
- **Use free hosting platforms** like Wix or Shopify
- **SEO tricks** to appear in Google search results (Search Engine Optimisation)
- **Using paid Google ads,** or social media ads, to appear legitimate

Safe Browsing Habits

Here's how to shop, bank, and browse confidently:

✓ Favourite / Bookmark any official sites that you use frequently
✓ Never click login links within emails - type the URL yourself in to your browser
✓ Use a password manager app to autofill passwords - they recognise the real site/s
✓ Shop on sites with legitimate contact information, reviews, and refund policies
✓ Avoid deals that seem way too good to be true

✓ Only donate money through well-known, verified platforms

Summary

Fake websites are everywhere - and getting better at deceiving us. But with a few simple habits and a trained eye, you can spot the fakes before they cause damage.

It's not about being paranoid - it's about being alert.

CHAPTER EIGHT

Malware, Viruses & Trojans - How Hackers Hijack Your Devices

"A single click can cost a company millions or lock your photos and documents forever."

We've all heard the words **virus, malware, spyware, Trojan, ransomware** - but what do they actually mean? Are they different? And more importantly, how do you prevent them from infecting your computer, phone, or even smart home?

In this chapter, we'll explore:
- The different types of malicious software
- How infections happen in the real world
- What damage they can do
- How to protect yourself on Windows, Mac, and mobile devices
- What to do if you think you've been infected

Let's start with the basics.

What Is Malware?
Malware (short for *malicious software*) is any software

created with the intention to:

- Damage your system
- Steal or lock your information
- Spy on your activity
- Hijack your resources
- Exploit your identity or finances

While terms like "virus" and "Trojan" are often used interchangeably, they are both actually **types of malware** - each with different behaviours and methods of spreading.

Types of Malware

Here is a list of the more common types of malware, what it does to your devices and what common symptoms to look for:

Virus - Infects files and spreads between systems. (Slow performance, random errors)

Worm - Self-replicates and spreads without human action (Network slowdowns)

Trojan - Disguises itself as a legit program to gain access (Data theft, backdoors)

Ransomware - Locks your files and demands payment (Files encrypted, ransom message)

Spyware - Secretly monitors your activity (Pop-ups, stolen logins)

Adware - Bombards you with unwanted ads (Endless pop-ups or redirects)

Rootkit - Hides deep in the system to allow remote access (Almost invisible)

Keylogger - Records every keystroke (Password theft, account compromise)

Botnet agent - Turns your device into a zombie for attackers (High CPU / network use)

Crypto miner - Uses your electricity to make money for someone else (High CPU / slow computer)

Each of these types of malware serves a different goal - but all of them are bad news.

How Malware Infects Devices

Here are some common infection methods in the wild:

1. Email Attachments and Links

- A fake invoice, CV, tracking notice or a fake document to sign lures you into clicking on the attachment.
- The attachment runs a hidden script when it is opened

2. Fake Software or Apps

- A "free" version of Photoshop, MS Office, or a game can contain a Trojan
- Mobile apps on third-party app stores or jailbroken / sideloaded APKs
- *An APK (Android Package Kit) is an app installer for Android - and sideloading is when you use developer mode to install that APK rather than downloading the app from the Google Store*

3. Infected Websites

- Known as **drive-by downloads**
- Simply visiting the page can trigger an invisible installation to happen

4. USB Drives

- Infected USBs (often dropped in parking lots and reception areas as bait) install malware automatically when plugged in

5. Pirated Media or Torrents
- Movies, music, or game cracks often come bundled with backdoors or spyware

6. Phishing Links
- A single wrong click gives malware a doorway into your system

Real-World Malware Attacks:

WannaCry (2017)
- Ransomware attack that hit hospitals, banks, and governments
- Exploited a Windows vulnerability
- It locked over 200,000 systems in 150+ countries
- Demanded Bitcoin payment

Emotet
- A powerful Trojan turned malware delivery system
- Spread via malicious email attachments
- Stole banking info and installed other types of malware

Pegasus Spyware
- High-end surveillance tool that infected phones via text (SMS), iMessage or a WhatsApp call (even if you didn't answer the call)
- Often used against journalists and activists, and usually used at a State-sponsored level as it is very expensive to purchase.

Toby or not Toby? That is the Question

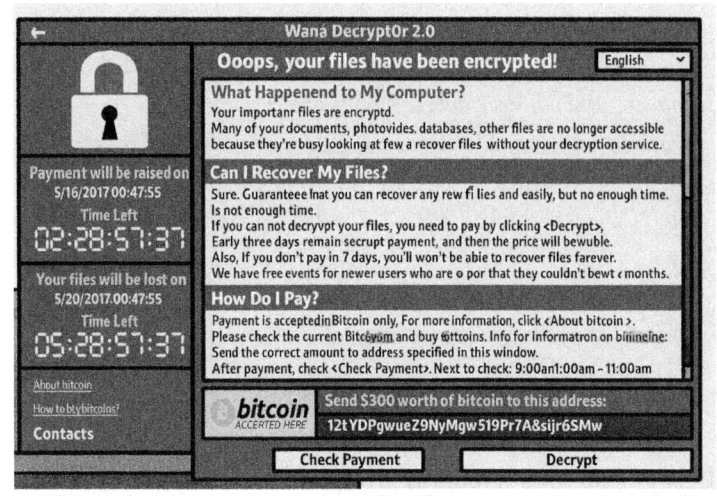

This is the payment pop-up window from a ransomware infection - in this case, the 2017 WannaCry outbreak.

What Malware Can Do to You

Once malware infects your system, it can do any one or more of these:

- Steal passwords, photos, or financial data
- Turn on your webcam or mic without your knowledge
- Encrypt your files and hold them for ransom
- Use your computer to mine cryptocurrency
- Launch attacks on others from your device (botnet)
- Monitor everything you type and view

And often, you won't even notice - until it's too late.

Signs You Might Be Infected

If you use your computer regularly then you will spot

most of these symptoms quite quickly:

Computer suddenly slow - Crypto mining, background tasks
Pop-ups and ads everywhere - Adware
Browser redirects - Hijacked browser or search settings

High CPU usage when idle - Malware processes

Programs you didn't install - Trojan, backdoor
Locked files with ransom message - Ransomware

Security software disabled - Rootkit or virus interference

If your antivirus suddenly disappears, or refuses to open - this is a major red flag.

How to Protect Your Devices

These 6 rules will help protect your devices against most threats - ask someone you trust, or a local IT professional, for their help if you are unsure how to implement any of them:

✓ 1. Use Reputable Antivirus/Anti-Malware Software
- Windows: Microsoft Defender, Malwarebytes, Bitdefender, etc
- Mac: Malwarebytes, Sophos, Intego, Bitdefender, etc
- Android: Lookout, Norton, Bitdefender, etc
- Keep it updated and let it run real-time scans

✓ 2. Update Your Operating Systems and Apps Regularly
- Many malware strains exploit old vulnerabilities
- Enable auto-updates wherever possible

✓ 3. Don't Download Software from Untrusted Sources

- Stick to the official app stores
- Avoid pirated software, game cracks, and serial key generators

✓ 4. Be Careful with Email Attachments and Links
- Never open files from unknown senders
- Hover over links before clicking

✓ 5. Use a Standard User Account (Not Admin) on Your Computer
- If malware runs on a non-admin account, it has limited damage potential. This step will require some technical know-how, but basically you create a new computer user account and give it Admin permissions, then, using that new Admin account, you downgrade your normal (daily) computer account to have just "Standard User" permissions. Continue to work normally in your usual account and only use the new Admin account when you need to install or update apps/software.

✓ 6. Back Up Your Data Regularly
- Use external drives or cloud services to backup your files and photos
- If ransomware hits you, then your backups can save you

Cyber Hygiene - Daily Habits That Keep Malware Out

✓ Think before you click - Don't open sketchy attachments
✓ Update everything - Operating system, browser and apps
✓ Avoid pirated software - Cracked software is laced with Trojans
✓ Use strong, unique passwords - Malware loves weak

passwords
✓ **Enable two-factor authentication (2FA)** - For extra protection
✓ **Back up regularly** - To the cloud or to an external drive
✓ **Use a reputable antivirus programme** - And keep it updated

The PDF That Cost $100,000

A small business accountant received a routine-looking email from a vendor with a PDF invoice. She opened it without hesitation.

What she didn't know was that the PDF contained a hidden script. Within minutes, ransomware began encrypting the company's shared drive.

The business didn't have proper backups. **They paid $100,000 in Bitcoin to get their files back.**

The attacker was a teenager in Eastern Europe - using a malware kit he bought online for $40.

What Is a "Zero-Day" Attack?

A **Zero-Day vulnerability** is a flaw in software that's unknown to the vendor and antivirus companies - and is therefore unpatched.

Hackers love Zero-Day vulnerabilities because:
- There's no fix available yet
- Antivirus doesn't detect it initially
- These exploits can be sold for millions on the dark web

Keeping your operating system and apps updated helps

reduce your exposure to these types of risks.

Tools Worth Having

Computer operating systems, including Windows 10 and newer, and macOS 10.8 and newer, all come with built-in malware protection - but many people still prefer to install their own preferred brand of malware programme.

The Windows and Mac default malware protection is good enough for most people - in fact, the UK Government's Cyber Essentials scheme states that it is sufficient to have the default malware protection enabled on your computer as long as you also ensure that all operating system and app updates are installed within 2-weeks of their release.

Some popular alternatives to the built-in protection are:

Malwarebytes - Deep scans your device for malware and PUPs*

Kaspersky Virus Removal Tool - Free cleanup utility

Bitdefender - Lightweight, real-time malware protection

A PUP is a "Potentially Unwanted Program", i.e. an app that malware installed on your computer without you knowing.

What to Do If You're Infected

If unsure how to do any of these, then use a different computer, phone or tablet to search the Internet for readily available instructions.

1. **Disconnect from the internet immediately**
2. **Boot into Safe Mode** - this restricts any malware activity
3. **Run a full system scan** with a trusted antivirus or

malware cleaner
4. **Change your passwords** by using a different device
5. **Check for strange programs or settings**
6. **Restore from a clean backup** if necessary
7. **Reinstall your operating system** if necessary - although, usually a last resort

If you're still unsure, get help from a local tech support professional or a trusted friend with IT knowledge.

Mobile Malware Warning

Yes, phones can get malware too - especially Android devices.

Android Phones and Tablets:
✗ Avoid...
- APK sideloading, especially from unknown sources
- Clicking suspicious links in SMS or DM's
- Allowing 'full access' to shady apps (such as to Contacts, SMS, Camera, etc.)

iPhones:
iPhones are at much less of a risk due to Apple's secure design, but not invincible. Avoid jailbreaking your iPhone, and keep your iOS and apps updated.

For Businesses and Remote Workers
Your employer should have strict computer use and security policies which you must adhere to, I would expect those policies to include all of these points:

- Use company-approved antivirus and VPN software / apps
- Never install unauthorised software / apps

- Don't use personal USB memory sticks or drives
- Lock your computer screen when away from your desk
- Keep backups off-network (to avoid ransomware spread)

Summary

Malware is everywhere - and it's no longer just about catching viruses from floppy disks. Today's threats are smarter, sneakier, and more financially motivated. But you don't need to be paranoid - just prepared.

- Stay updated
- Use strong protection
- Be cautious with what you click and install

A clean system is a safe system. And prevention is always cheaper than recovery.

CHAPTER NINE

Social Media Scams & Impersonation - Trust and Deceit in the Digital Age

"If it looks like your friend and reads like your friend, but they ask you for money - it very well might not be your friend!"

Social media has become the digital heartbeat of our personal lives - a place to connect, share, and belong. But for scammers, it's a **goldmine of trust, information, and access**. The platforms we use to stay in touch can also be used by scammers for manipulation, impersonation, and theft.

This chapter unpacks:
- Common social media scams and how they work
- How impersonation is used to manipulate victims
- The dangers of oversharing
- Best practices to lock down your accounts
- How to help others avoid falling victim

Why Social Media Is So Attractive to Scammers

1. **People let their guard down.** You trust who you're connected with.

2. **It's rich with personal data.** Birthdays, locations, family names, jobs, school names - all ideal for social engineering.
3. **Accounts are easy to impersonate (clone) or hijack.**
4. **Scammers can reach hundreds of people instantly.**

It's not just about hacking - it's about **exploiting trust**. And the tactics evolve constantly.

Common Social Media Scams

1. Impersonation Scams
- A scammer clones someone's profile (same name, photo and mutual friends)
- They message people pretending to be that person

Requests include things like:
- "I'm locked out of my bank - can you send me £100?"
- "I need a passcode, can I send it to your phone number?"
- "Check out this crazy video of you!"

Real-world case: A woman in the UK was tricked into wiring £2,500 to someone she thought was her daughter on Instagram. It was a clone account.

If a scammer clones your account, it doesn't mean they have hacked their way in to it - rather, cloning simply means that they have created a new social media account and copied your name and profile picture. No hacking involved.

2. Phishing Links - "Clickbait" Traps
- "Is this you in this video?" and a link - leads to a fake login page
- You enter your credentials and your credentials are

stolen instantly
Often shared through:
- Facebook Messenger
- Instagram Direct Messages (DMs)
- TikTok DM's
- WhatsApp and Telegram messages

3. Investment or "Crypto Flipping" Scams
- "I turned £300 into £5,000 in a week!" - accompanied by fake screenshots
- They offer to "invest" on your behalf
- You send money or crypto - and never hear back

Often promoted via:
- Instagram Stories and Adverts, often with fake celebrity endorsements
- X / Twitter through both normal messages and DMs
- Fake "verified-looking" influencer accounts and cloned financial advisors

4. Giveaway or Contest Scams
- "Congratulations! You won a prize!" from a page that looks like a real brand
- They ask for a "processing fee" or personal details
- Sometimes, the links lead to malware or phishing pages
- Often when a big brand runs a competition, dozens of fake, similarly named accounts suddenly get made by scammers who then try to con those who entered the competition.

Watch for fake handles like:
- @CocaCola__Official instead of @CocaCola
- @NikePromo.2024 instead of @Nike

5. Romance & Relationship Scams
We covered this in detail in a previous chapter, but many romance scams do **start on social media** rather than on dating apps - especially fake celebrity ones saying things along these lines; "this is my secret second account" or "this account is for my special fans only"

6. Charity or Disaster Relief Scams
- Fake GoFundMe pages
- Stolen images of sick, hungry children or disaster victims
- Emotional manipulation and urgency - donations sent to scammers

7. Marketplace & Job Offer Scams
- Fake buyers on Facebook Marketplace: "I'll send a courier to collect it" and sending fake banking payment screenshots.
- Fake job offers on LinkedIn or Instagram: "Work from home! £500 per day!"

The Art of Impersonation
Scammers impersonate:
- Friends or family
- Influencers or brands
- Tech support agents or banking security teams
- Government, tax or financial agencies

How do they do it?
- They clone profiles which have publicly visible information
- Copy profile photos, captions, hashtags
- Add mutual friends to appear legitimate

Then they **reach out and manipulate**:
- "I need help"
- "I got locked out of my account - can you verify this code?"
- "Check out this opportunity I just got"

One of the attempted crypto investment scams I see quite a lot on social media happens just after **you follow a well known financial advisor**, an accountant or an investment expert - suddenly, you start to get identical looking, similarly named accounts follow you. Except on close inspection they are clones of the real financial account that you just followed. These **cloned accounts will strike up a conversation in DM's** claiming to be genuine (i.e. "This is my backup account") and, of course, the next thing you know they are **asking you if you want to put money in to their crypto investment scheme**. It's a scam - a very obvious one, but many social media platforms don't recognise it as a scam when you report it, and they allow the scammers to continue to operate.

Remember, if it feels off - it probably is.

Red Flags to Watch For

Here are some key points to look out for, however, bear in mind that new scammer techniques appear all the time:

✗ *New account with just a few posts but many followers* - Likely a fake or bought account

✗ *DM from a friend asking for money* - Could be impersonation or hijacking

✗ *Messages with only a link and no context* - Classic phishing attempt

✗ *Requests for 2FA codes* - Someone's trying to hijack your account

✗ *Friend requests from someone you're already connected with* - A cloned account

✗ *Influencer asking for crypto* - Likely scam, even if verified-looking

How to Protect Yourself

✓ 1. Set Accounts to Private (Wherever Possible)
- Only approve people you know
- It prevent scammers from scraping your photos or details

✓ 2. Use Two-Factor Authentication (2FA)
- Use an app (like Google or Microsoft Authenticator) - not just SMS
- Enable it on all platforms: Facebook, Instagram, X (Twitter), LinkedIn, etc

✓ 3. Be Careful What You Post

Don't share information such as this:
- Pet names (common password elements)
- Mother's maiden name
- Birth year
- Vacation plans (in case it invites break-ins or scams)
- School uniform photos or your work ID
- Use generic captions and avoid detailed personal info

✓ 4. Check Social Media @'s (Handles) Carefully
- Look for spelling differences, extra punctuation, odd characters
- Verified accounts are safer - but not foolproof

✓ 5. Use Unique Passwords for Each Platform
- Use a password manager (Bitwarden, 1Password, etc.)
- If one platform is breached, others stay safe when you have unique passwords

What to Do If You're Targeted

If your account is compromised:
- Change your password immediately
- Revoke access to suspicious apps (search online on how to do this)
- Alert your contacts
- Report the issue to the platform

If you spot a clone account:
- Report it as impersonation
- Warn others not to engage
- Screenshot for evidence (if needed)

Protecting the Vulnerable

Scammers often target:
- Seniors
- Teenagers
- People that are less tech-savvy

If you know someone at risk:
- Help them lock down privacy settings
- Educate them on phishing and fake profiles
- Encourage them to double-check unusual messages

Good Habits for Social Media Safety

Social media can be a minefield for scams and false information, here are some helpful habits you may like to take on board going forward:

Review privacy settings monthly - Platforms change defaults settings often

Regularly check your login activity - Spot unknown devices on your account

Don't reuse old passwords - Prevents further hacking

Avoid quizzes like "Which Disney character are you?" - They are often used for data mining

Pause before clicking - A second of doubt can prevent days of regret

Platform-Specific Advice

Each social media platform (app or site) has slightly different settings, here are some of the main ones you should check and change if necessary:

Facebook:
- Enable login alerts
- Limit who can look you up using your phone or

- email
- Review app permissions (Settings > Apps and Websites)

Instagram:
- Turn on 2FA
- Be wary of DM links and "we want you to be an ambassador" invites
- Report impersonators quickly

TikTok:
- Use phone / email login for better control
- Avoid DMs from strangers offering money or intimate photos
- Avoid "celebs" replying to your comments saying "this is my personal account, DM me as I have something you may be interested in"
- Be aware of any accounts that DM you and start talking about crypto investments

LinkedIn:
- Be sceptical of job offers that ask for upfront fees or crypto
- Don't accept every connection request, take a moment to check their profile first

Resources and Reporting

Each platform has their own reporting mechanism, but if you have ever tried reporting accounts or posts you will know it can be quite hit-and-miss as to whether the platform will take the appropriate action. Blocking scam accounts, as well as offensive and deceptive accounts, after you have reported them is a definite must. Reporting pages:

Facebook - facebook.com/help/reportlinks
Instagram - instagram.com/hacked
X / Twitter - help.x.com/en/forms
TikTok - Report through in-app options
LinkedIn - linkedin.com/help

For phishing links or serious fraud:
- actionfraud.police.uk (UK)
- ftc.gov (USA)
- scamwatch.gov.au (Australia)

Summary

Social media brings us closer, but it also opens us up to deception. Scammers use our trust, our connections, and our emotions to bypass our usual defences.

But awareness is your best armour:
- Be sceptical of sudden messages or offers
- Guard your personal info
- Lock down your profiles and enable 2FA

If something feels too urgent, emotional, or easy - pause. Real friends don't pressure you.

CHAPTER TEN

Passwords, Authentication & Identity Theft - Securing the Keys to Your Digital Life

"A weak password is like a cheap padlock - it might look strong, but anyone can open it with a paperclip."

Your password is often the only thing standing between a cybercriminal and your money, your photos, your communications, and your identity. Yet many people still use passwords like 123456, qwerty, or password.

In this chapter, we'll explore:
- Why passwords still matter (even when using biometrics and 2FA)
- How hackers crack them
- The anatomy of a strong password
- Password managers: why they're not scary
- Multi-Factor Authentication (MFA and 2FA) demystified
- The growing threat of identity theft

It can get a bit complex, but I will try to explain things as simply as I can.

Why Passwords Matter
Despite all the talk about facial recognition, fingerprint login, and magic links, **passwords are still currently the foundation of digital identity**.

- Your email password can be exploited to unlock every account you've ever registered using your email address.
- A single breached password can unlock banking, social media, cloud storage, and health data.
- Most online services still rely on a username and password combination as their primary gatekeeper.

Yet many people reuse the same password across multiple sites. That's like using the same key for your house, car, and office - and then leaving it under your doormat.

How Hackers Actually Steal Passwords
Let's look at the main attack methods:

1. Phishing
- You get a fake email from "Netflix" or "Microsoft"
- You're asked to "log in to confirm your account"
- You enter your password on a fake website - they steal it instantly

2. Credential Stuffing
- From a previous data breach - your email address and password are leaked online
- Hackers also try those same combinations of credentials on other platforms
- It works if you **reused the same password elsewhere**

3. Brute Force
- Automated tools try every possible combination of characters, very quickly
- Most effective when used on short or simple passwords

4. Dictionary Attacks
- Combines common words, names, and numbers like john1983, summer123
- Especially effective against personal passwords using birthdays, pet names, etc.

5. Social Engineering Example
- Your dog's name is Rocky - that info is visible on Instagram
- Your birth year is shown on Facebook - 1988
- Your password is Rocky1988 - a hacker knowing the above will guess it easily

The Most Common, Terrible Passwords

These come from a compiled list of several real data breaches - the full list of terrible passwords is extremely long, but these are the top 10 worst offenders:

- 123456
- password
- qwerty
- iloveyou
- admin
- welcome
- letmein
- abc123
- monkey
- football

These get cracked (brute-forced) by password guessing software in **a fraction of a second**.

What Makes a Strong Password?

A secure password will have the following characteristics:

✓ At least 12–16 characters
✓ A mix of uppercase, lowercase, numbers, and symbols
✓ No single dictionary words or personal info
✓ No repeated or sequential characters (1111, abcd)

Here is an example of what is traditionally considered a strong password:

M7!qvP@29z!LxR%

But this is going to be too hard to remember, so you may be tempted to write it down somewhere - that's where **passphrases** and **password managers** come in.

Use Passphrases Instead

They are easier to remember and still very secure - using passphrases is the current recommended method by multiple cybersecurity authorities around the world, here are a couple of examples:

Correct-Horse-Battery-Staple!
BlueBanana99!EagleSkate!

Pro Tips:
- Use four or more unrelated words
- Add numbers and symbols randomly
- Avoid quotes, song lyrics, or famous phrases

What Is a Password Manager? (And Why You Need One)

A password manager app is like a **vault** for all your passwords. It remembers them for you and can generate strong new ones if needed. Information kept in a password manager is securely encrypted.

Popular app options:
- Bitwarden (free and open-source)
- 1Password
- Dashlane
- NordPass
- iCloud Keychain (Apple devices only)

Benefits:
- Can auto-fill logins securely if you opt to have it do so
- Stores unique passwords on a per site basis and knows if a site is legit
- Encrypted database, with a strong master password

Using the same password everywhere is convenient… **until it gets you hacked.**

What Is Two-Factor Authentication (2FA/MFA)?

Cyber professionals will be all to familiar with the phrase "Something you know, something you have, and something you are":

Something you know - a password, PIN number or a security question

Something you have - a mobile device generating single-use codes, a USB security token or a smart-card

Something you are - biometrics, such as a fingerprint, facial recognition, iris recognition or your voice pattern.

Two-factor authentication, also **known as 2FA**, means to require the use of any two of the above categories.

Most of us are familiar with the single-use **passcodes that get sent to your phone** when logging in to banking or other secure sites - this is what is most commonly referred to as Two-Factor Authentication (2FA). There is also Multi-Factor Authentication (MFA), technically it is slightly different to 2FA, but you will often hear both terms used interchangeably.

Types of 2FA:
- **Text messages (SMS)** - better than nothing, but not ideal due to the possibility of SIM swapping (similar to hijacking your phone number)
- **Authenticator apps** - such as Google Authenticator and Microsoft Authenticator are much more secure than using text messages.
- **Hardware tokens** - like YubiKey, are physical devices, used for ultra-secure accounts, which must be plugged in to the USB port of your computer in order for you to log in. People working in a high-security job may have to use these.
- **Biometrics** (face/fingerprint) - are secure and fast, and with recent support for PassKeys on mobile devices this is becoming more common. PassKeys are a cryptographic method of verifying your identity, using your biometrics, when you log in to a website or app. They are very secure, much more secure than using passwords, and PassKeys are going to be the

way forward.

Always enable 2FA on these types of platforms:
- Email - such as Gmail, Outlook and iCloud. (Note, not all email services support 2FA at this time - check your email provider's FAQ page to see if they do)
- Banking apps - most banking apps have compulsory 2FA nowadays
- Social media - protect your social media accounts against being hijacked
- Cloud storage - such as Dropbox, Google Drive, iCloud, etc

Identity Theft: Beyond Just Passwords

Identity theft is when someone steals your **personal information** to:

- Open credit accounts in your name
- Masquerade as you to set up a company
- Stalk and harass people whilst pretending to be you
- Commit crimes pretending to be you

Information frequently stolen includes:
- Full name and address
- Date of birth
- Driver's license number
- Phone number
- Account credentials
- Government ID number (National Insurance number, Social Security Number, passport, etc)

How it's done:
- Data breaches of companies who hold your data
- Malware or keyloggers installed on your computer

- Phishing via email or messaging
- Buying data on the dark web - fresh data breaches for sale
- Old-fashioned sifting through your rubbish - 'Dumpster Diving'

Be Careful With Your ID (and Theirs)

If you send your ID documents, such as your driving licence or passport, to someone who turns out to be a scammer, then **you have just handed a criminal some of your most valuable and useful data** - a Government issued photo-ID with all of your details on, including your full name, date of birth, home address and your signature.

Many scammers will ask you to send proof of your identity as part of their masquerade, especially if it is a financial or crypto investment scam. Hopefully though, by this point your will have spotted the warning signs and you don't proceed any further.

One red flag to look out for is that **a legitimate business will never ask you to send identity documents by email** - a legitimate company will have an official website with a secure document upload facility (sending documents by email is insecure).

Below is a replica of an actual driving licence being used by a scammer, as proof of his own identity, it is from one of the cases I recently investigated - no great surprise, but it is fake. In this case, **the scammer has actually repurposed the real driving licence of one of their previous victims** - using photo editing software they have changed the photo, date of birth and the first 5 digits of the driving licence number.

How do I know this is fake? Firstly, a reverse image search reveals the person's photo to be that of a model used in many stock photos; readily available on the Internet. But for me **as an investigator, the driving licence number is a huge giveaway**.

A UK driving licence number is structured in a specific way and is based on the driver's name, date of birth and sex - in this case I can tell the original licence was issued to a female born on the 16th December 1955 whose first name begins with the letter K.

The scammer only **changed the first 5 characters** of the licence number so it matched his surname (ROZMA), but left the rest of the number as it was - in fact, they even left the previous victim's home address on the licence (the part I've censored).

```
UK  DRIVING LICENCE
     1. ROZMAN
     2. MR THOMAS
     3. 12.02.1991  UNITED KINGDOM
     4a. 19.05.2021  DVLA
     4b. 15.12.2025
     5. ROZMA562165K988A  11
     8. ▓▓▓▓▓ ROAD, STOKE-ON-TRENT, ▓▓▓
     9. ▓▓▓▓▓▓▓▓▓▓▓▓▓▓▓▓▓▓▓▓▓▓
AM/A/B1/C1/D1/BE/C1E/D1E/f/k//l/n/pq
```

Your photo-ID could end up being used in the same way if you inadvertently send it to a criminal, or worse - you could become the victim of identity theft as they rack up thousands of pounds worth of debt in your name.

The Cost of Identity Theft

Depending on your data source the financial figures can vary significantly - it isn't just about money though; there is reputational damage to consider as well as any delays and possibly even a tax or police investigation to deal with. These are some of the types of loss we frequently see:

Credit fraud - £204 (UK), $500–$2,000 (US)

Tax fraud or Company fraud - Delays, investigations, hours lost

Bank fraud - May drain you full bank account

Reputation damage - Social & professional fallout

How to Detect Identity Theft

If you have banking apps and credit card apps installed on your phone, you can instantly receive notifications on your phone and see any strange transactions.

Signs of identity theft include:
- Charges on your credit or debit card that you don't recognise
- Calls about loans or debts you know nothing about
- Unexpected or unknown bills or contracts arriving in the post
- Suspicious login alerts from websites

How to Protect Your Identity

✓ 1. Use Strong, Unique Passwords (and a Password Manager)

- Don't reuse passwords, even for "unimportant" sites

✓ 2. Lock Down Personal Info Online
- Remove birthdates, addresses, family info from public social media profiles
- Avoid quizzes and surveys that collect personal details

✓ 3. Shred Physical Documents
- Don't throw out intact tax records, bills, card or bank statements. Shred them

✓ 4. Use 2FA Everywhere You Can

✓ 5. Register with a credit monitoring service
- Such as Experian, Equifax or for free with Credit Karma

✓ 6. Freeze Your Credit (US)
- Prevents criminals from opening new accounts in your name
- Free via Experian, Equifax, and TransUnion

What to Do If You're a Victim

1. **Change all passwords immediately**
2. **Enable 2FA on all accounts**
3. **Check for unauthorised transactions or accounts being opened**
4. **Report to authorities:**
    - UK: actionfraud.police.uk
    - US: identitytheft.gov
    - AUS: scamwatch.gov.au
6. **Freeze your credit (US), and alert your bank and**

card providers
7. **Register with a credit monitoring service if you haven't already done so**

Summary

In today's world, your **password is your first line of defence** - but it's not enough by itself. Strong passwords, smart habits, and layered authentication are essential to protecting your identity.

Key Takeaways:
- Use a password manager
- Enable 2FA on all important accounts
- Stay alert to phishing and data breaches

Your data is worth protecting - because it's more than data. It's your life.

CHAPTER ELEVEN

Wi-Fi Home & Public Networks - Defending Your Digital Perimeter

"If your Wi-Fi isn't secured it can be like leaving your front door unlocked."

Wi-Fi networks, both at home and on the go, act like a digital front door. If it's insecure, anyone with a bit of know-how can sneak in, snoop on your activity, steal your credentials, or even install malware.

In the UK, your WiFi router may have been supplied by your broadband provider, as most are, in which case it should already be secure and correctly locked down, so **this chapter may not apply to you**. But in other countries, or where you've purchased and installed the router yourself, then the below may still apply.

A few years ago, I was remotely assisting my father, who lived in the US, with a computer problem and I was shocked to find that his Wi-Fi name (known as the SSID) was set to be the same as his home phone number - this was how it was supplied and installed by his broadband provider. So, without him realising, he was advertising his phone number to everyone within Wi-Fi range - additionally, in the US, knowing somebody's phone number opens up ways for anyone, including scammers, to find out the property details and occupier's name. Fortunately this is more of a localised risk, but it is still rather concerning.

In this chapter, we'll walk through:
- The risks of using public Wi-Fi (airports, cafes, hotels)
- How cybercriminals intercept data on shared networks
- What a VPN really does (and doesn't do)
- Wi-Fi security myths vs. facts

Why Wi-Fi Security Matters
Even if your laptop is configured securely, using an unsecured Wi-Fi network can render those defences useless.

Here are a few key points to start:
- Hackers target weak Wi-Fi encryption, default passwords and open networks
- Public Wi-Fi hotspots can be spoofed - imitated or cloned
- Your data is at risk in transit - passwords, messages, emails, banking logins, etc

Cybersecurity professionals will be familiar with the phrase **"data in transit",** and its sister-phrase **"data at rest"** - A simple explanation would be, whilst you are downloading an email, it is in transit (hence "Data in Transit") and once the email has finished downloading, it will be sitting at rest in your inbox ("Data at Rest").

Data in transit needs to be securely encrypted as it moves

across networks and the Internet to prevent digital-eavesdropping, and some of that responsibility lies with the configuration of the Wi-Fi network.

The Dangers of Public Wi-Fi

You're sitting at a café and connect to "Free_Coffee_WiFi." That seems harmless, right?

But how do you know:
- Who set it up?
- Whether it's properly encrypted?
- Whether it's a rogue hotspot designed to harvest your data or activity?

Scammers often sit in public areas, like a coffee shop, and have their laptop set up to mimic the coffee shop's Wi-Fi name. Here are the 4 most common of these types of attack on public networks:

1. *Man-in-the-Middle (MITM) Attacks*
 - Hacker intercepts your data in transit, between your device and the website
 - They create a stronger Wi-Fi signal of the same name - your device connects to it
 - The hacker can capture some of your logins, emails or messages in real-time

2. *Evil Twin Hotspots*
 - Fake Wi-Fi with a familiar name (e.g., "Starbucks_WiFi")
 - You connect, thinking it's legitimate and the hacker captures everything you do

3. *Packet Sniffing*
 - Advanced tools like Wireshark or Aircrack-ng can read unencrypted Wi-Fi traffic
 - Even HTTPS web traffic can leak metadata, URLs, and login attempts

4. *Malware Injection*
 - Some rogue networks will redirect you to fake sites that install malware

Rule of thumb: Don't log in to sensitive accounts (banking, work or email) when using public Wi-Fi, unless you're using a VPN.

How to Use Public Wi-Fi Safely

My personal approach is to never use public Wi-Fi - instead, I tether my laptop to my phone's own Wi-Fi hotspot. However there are some occasions where there is no mobile phone signal and instead I fire-up my VPN and connect to the public Wi-Fi:

✓ *Use a VPN* - A VPN app encrypts all traffic between your device and the internet

✓ *Only visit HTTPS sites* - Secure websites have end-to-end encryption, which prevents snooping. Most sites use HTTPS nowadays

✓ *Disable auto-connect to networks* - Stops your phone from inadvertently connecting to dangerous hotspots

✓ *Turn off file/printer sharing* - Blocks unauthorised access to files on your computer

✓ *Turn on your device's firewall* - Most computers nowadays have this turned on by default.

✓ *Keep your operating system and antivirus up to date* - Prevents exploitation of known vulnerabilities

✗ *Don't access banking or email unless needed* - Save it for when on a trusted, secure network

✗ *Don't log in to sites without 2FA* - 2FA adds a critical layer of protection

Step-by-Step Home Wi-Fi Security Checklist (Very Advanced)

As mentioned above, if you are in the UK and your broadband supplier provided the router, then you will find all of these recommendations should already be in place and you can skip over this section. (In other countries, broadband routers may also come pre-configured).

If you purchased your own Wi-Fi router, or your broadband provider has supplied you with an insecurely configured router, then you can make these changes via the router's admin console - it is fairly advanced, so you may need to ask someone to help you with this:

1. **Change your router's default admin username & password**
   - Hackers use lists of default credentials (such as U: admin P: admin)

2. **Use WPA3 encryption if available**
   - WPA2 is acceptable; but WEP is completely outdated
   - You'll find this setting in your router's admin console

3. **Use a long, strong Wi-Fi password**
   - Mix upper and lowercase letters, numbers and symbols
   - Example: HomeNet_57!A3k@Secure

4. **Rename your network SSID**
   - Avoid default names like "Linksys123" or "TP-Link"
   - Don't use personal info like your name or addresses or telephone number

5. **Disable WPS (Wi-Fi Protected Setup)**
   - It's a physical vulnerability, turn WPS off if you don't need to use it

6. **Create a separate Guest Network (if possible)**
   - Keep guests isolated from your main devices if your router supports this

7. **Update your router firmware regularly if you provided it yourself**
   - Just like your phone or computer, routers get security patches too
   - Most routers provided by your ISP will auto-update their firmware.

8. **Turn off remote administration**
 - Unless you really need it, remote access just opens a door for attackers
 - Most newer routers will have this feature disabled by default

What Is a VPN? And Do You Need One?
A **VPN (Virtual Private Network)** encrypts all of your Internet activity and routes it through a secure server, simultaneously protecting your data (in transit) and also hiding your location.

Benefits:
 - Prevents local snooping by hackers (for example, when on public Wi-Fi)
 - Hides your IP address from websites that you access
 - Bypasses geographical-restrictions for sites and streaming services.

Limitations:
 - Doesn't protect you from phishing or malware
 - Doesn't make you anonymous from websites you log into
 - The VPN provider could possibly see your data - so choose a provider carefully

Recommended VPNs:
 - ProtonVPN (trusted, secure, offers free tier)
 - NordVPN, Surfshark, ExpressVPN (user-friendly, fast)
 - Mullvad (no personal data, privacy-focused)

Use a VPN especially when travelling, working remotely, or using public Wi-Fi. Be aware that some free VPN's are known to monitor what you do, or route traffic through China without the users knowledge. To minimise risk, use a paid VPN if you can, and avoid the free ones.

Summary

Your internet security is only as strong as your weakest connection. Whether you're at home or using a café's free Wi-Fi, the risks are real - but manageable with a few smart habits.

- Avoid public Wi-Fi for sensitive tasks
- Use a VPN when needed

You lock your doors at night. Now lock your network too.

CHAPTER TWELVE

Children, Teens & Online Safety - Raising Cyber-Smart Kids

"Like elephants, the Internet never forgets. Teach kids how to navigate it safely."

As children grow up immersed in the digital world, they're faced with risks and opportunities previous generations never imagined. From YouTube to gaming platforms, Discord servers, school chats to social media, the online world is their playground, classroom, and social scene - all at once.

In this chapter, I'll help you understand:
- The unique online risks children and teens face
- Practical ways to guide, monitor, and protect them
- Common scams, predators, and pitfalls targeting young users
- Tools and parental controls that work
- How to talk about online privacy, reputation, and digital citizenship

Let's dive straight in - no scare tactics, just facts and cyber-savvy guidance.

Why Are Children Targets of Cybercriminals?

Children spend a lot of time online and the platforms they chat and play on are well known to cybercriminals - quite often the young don't have the necessary experience to quickly assess and identify a threat, and when they do, it can sometimes be too late.

For example:
- Children trust people quite easily
- They often lack awareness of scams or risks
- They leave large digital footprints without realising it
- Once their identity (personal information) is stolen, **it can be abused for years before anyone notices**

Teens are also especially vulnerable to:
- Online grooming and predators
- Sextortion - both real and AI generated
- Reputation damage from oversharing
- Cyberbullying and harassment
- Addiction and screen fatigue

Common Threats to Children Online

1. Online Predators
- Often pretend to be another child or teen
- Try to lure kids away from gaming or chat platforms to other private chats
- Attempt to build trust and later ask for inappropriate and illegal content

Teach your child to:
- Never share personal info (school, address, their full name, etc)

- Report and block anyone asking for photos or secret meetings or chats
- Come to you if anything feels weird or uncomfortable - and with no punishment
- Never send or share photos with anyone, even if they think they are friends

2. Cyberbullying
- Happens on messaging apps, gaming platforms, social media, and more
- Includes harassment, exclusion, public shaming, threats
- Kids may hide it from you out of shame or fear

What to do:
- Encourage open communication
- Keep records and screenshots of any abuse
- Report it to the platform (and to the school if needed)
- Remind them it's okay to block people and to leave toxic spaces

3. Inappropriate Content
- Easily accessible on platforms like Reddit, Discord, or even YouTube
- Includes violence, pornography, hate speech and extremism
- It may show up as ads, suggested content, or links sent by others

How to reduce exposure:
- Enable **Safe Search** on their Google account if they have one
- Use **YouTube Kids** (which has age-appropriate content)
- Monitor their app installations and use **content filters/apps**

- Set age restrictions on platforms like Netflix, TikTok, Xbox, etc

4. Scams & Phishing
- "You've won 10,000 Robux!"
- Fake Fortnite skins or free V-Bucks
- Beware phishing links in chats promising free prizes or followers

Teach them:
- Nothing is free - if it seems too good to be true, it is
- Never give out personal details, usernames, passwords, or codes
- Ask before clicking on anything that is unfamiliar

5. Overexposure & Reputation Damage
- Teens may post personal photos, details, or opinions which they later regret
- These posts can be saved, screenshotted, or shared indefinitely

Discuss:
- The concept of a "digital footprint"
- How colleges, future employers and bullies can access old posts and content
- The value of privacy settings and using private accounts

Guiding Your Child's Digital Life - Age by Age

Ages 3–7:
- - Use parent-controlled devices
- - Only pre-approved apps or games
- - Stay nearby during their use
- - Use "kid mode" apps. Most app stores give age ratings (YouTube Kids, etc)

Ages 8–12:
- - Begin teaching internet safety basics
- - Set screen time limits and use parental control apps
- - Co-view content and discuss what they're watching
- - Encourage critical thinking - for example, "Is that advert real?"

Ages 13–17:
- - Respect growing independence, but discuss boundaries
- - Talk openly about cyberbullying, sexting, and peer pressure
- - Encourage critical thinking about followers, likes, and influence
- - Help them understand digital permanence

Tools & Parental Controls That Work

Below are a few examples of Parental Control apps. There are quite a lot of different Parental Control apps and services available, take some time and do your research online and find the one that best suits your requirements, and that is compatible with your devices. Here are some tools to consider:

Bark - Monitors messages, alerts parents to risks
Qustodio - Time limits, app blocking, activity reports
Google Family Link - Free, app controls and monitoring
Apple Screen Time - Built-in on iPhones and iPads
Microsoft Family Safety - Great for Windows/Xbox users

Choose tools that match both your child's age and your tech comfort level.

Have "The Talk" - Digital Edition

Just like you'd talk about crossing the street or being aware of strangers, talk with your children about online safety - do so regularly as technology and dangers do change frequently.

Here are key points to cover:
- - "If someone makes you uncomfortable, tell me - you won't get in trouble."
- - "Anything you post can be copied and shared forever."
- - "Not everyone online is who they say they are."
- - "You don't have to respond to bullies. You can always block or report them."

This isn't a one-time talk - it's an ongoing conversation as your child grows and technology evolves.

Digital Responsibility

Teach children that being online comes with responsibility.

- Be respectful and kind
- Don't share things that hurt others
- Question sources before believing or sharing
- Protect personal info like passwords and photos
- Report anything harmful or suspicious
- Teach them to pause before posting: "Would I be okay if my mum, my teacher, and my future boss saw this?"

What to Do If Something Goes Wrong

What should you do if your child...
- Encounters a predator

- Is cyberbullied
- Shares inappropriate content
- Falls for a scam or downloads malware

Here's what to do:
1. Stay calm. Focus on safety, not blame.
2. Talk with them. Ask what happened and how they feel.
3. Secure their devices. Run anti-malware scans or reset them as needed.
4. Report using the in-app tools, talk to schools and involve authorities if necessary.
5. Educate - use the moment as a learning opportunity.

Summary

Your child's digital life is rich, complicated, and evolving. With the right guidance, tools, and trust, they can explore it safely.

Key Takeaways:
- Know the apps and platforms your child uses
- Use filters, controls, and monitoring wisely - not secretly
- Keep communication open - no judgment, just safety
- Teach kids to think critically, act kindly, and protect their privacy

The Internet is powerful. So is a well-informed child.

CHAPTER THIRTEEN

Sextortion - Fear, Shame, and Digital Blackmail

"They trick you into silence. That's their power."

Sextortion is one of the most emotionally devastating forms of online crime. It combines hacking, manipulation, and blackmail - with a uniquely cruel weapon: shame.

Whether it begins with flirtation, hacking, or deepfake images, sextortion cases are rising across every age group. And unlike other scams, victims often don't report it - out of fear, guilt, or embarrassment.

In this chapter, we break down how sextortion works, how to spot it, what to do if you or someone you know is targeted - and how to prevent it altogether.

What Is Sextortion?

Sextortion is the use of sexual imagery - real or fabricated - to extort money, favours, or silence from a victim.

It typically involves:
- A scammer or hacker obtaining private photos or

videos
- Threatening to release them publicly to friends, family and on social media
- Demanding money and / or more images, or continued contact

Sometimes, the images are real, taken during online chats or stolen from devices. Other times, they're deepfakes - AI-generated from innocent photos.

How It Begins: Common Sextortion Scenarios

1. Flirt-Then-Blackmail Trap
- Scammer contacts their target on social media, a game chat or dating app
- Conversation rapidly escalates into sexual chat or video calls
- Victim is encouraged to send explicit photos or videos
- Sometimes the scammer asks for seemingly innocent photos at the beginning
- Then comes: "Send me money, or I'll send these to your family and contacts"

2. Hacked Account / Webcam Attack
- Scammer claims to have hacked your device or webcam
- May show your password or past messages to seem legitimate
- Threatens to release recordings unless you're cooperative
- Often these claims are false and designed to trick you in to sending images

3. Deepfake Sextortion
- Uses AI to fabricate sexually explicit images/videos of you from public photos
- Sends samples and says, "This is already online unless you pay us to remove it"

4. Underage Sextortion (very common and tragic)
- Teen is groomed by someone pretending to be a peer or romantic acquaintance
- The teen is talked in to sending a revealing or nude photo
- Blackmailer then threatens to send it to family and contacts unless more are sent
- This often escalates into relentless harassment
- The blackmailer will most often also ask for money to not share the images

What Sextortionists Rely On
Their weapon is **fear**, but there are things that you can do to take back control.

They rely on:
- Embarrassment keeping you from telling someone
- Emotional panic overriding rational action
- Victims acting alone, under pressure
- The hope that you'll pay - quickly, and quietly

If You Are Targeted: Do This Immediately

1. Do Not Respond or Pay
- Paying will not stop them - it encourages further demands
- Anything you say gives them control

2. Save All Evidence
- Screenshots of messages, usernames, images and timestamps
- Keep URLs, emails, and their contact info
- The authorities can use the evidence to identify the blackmailer

3. Block and Report
- Block the scammer on all platforms
- Report the account to the platform (e.g. Facebook, Instagram, Snapchat)

4. Tell Someone You Trust
- Shame shrinks when shared. You're not alone.
- A trusted friend, parent, teacher or counsellor can help you think clearly

5. Report to Authorities
- Police take sextortion very seriously - especially with minors involved
- In the UK: CEOP at www.ceop.police.uk/Safety-Centre
- In the U.S., you can also report to:
  - NCMEC CyberTipline
  - FBI's IC3
- Australia: eSafety.gov.au

6. Contact the Platform
- Most social platforms will remove non-consensual imagery
- You can also **use StopNCII.org to stop intimate content from being shared** or resurfacing

There are some additional resources and instructions to have images removed from each platform on the NCMEC website - it is a good idea to take some time to explore the information and instructions they give:

www.missingkids.org/gethelpnow/isyourexplicitcontentoutthere

How to Protect Yourself

✓ 1. Strengthen Device Security
- Use **strong passwords** and 2FA on all accounts
- Cover your webcam when not in use
- Use antivirus software and update your operating system regularly

✓ 2. Lock Down Social Media
- Make accounts **private**
- Be careful what you share publicly (photos, friends list, school, location)
- Avoid accepting friend requests from strangers

✓ 3. Be Cautious in Digital Intimacy
- If someone pushes for nudes or video chats **quickly**, it's a red flag
- Real relationships build trust slowly
- Assume anything shared online could be screen-recorded
- Sometimes scammers may start by asking for less-revealing images
- **Always assume what you share will be seen by others, not just by one person**

✓ 4. Watch for Deepfake Manipulation

- New tools can fabricate images using only a public selfie
- Check if your name is searchable with explicit images
- Use tools like Google's Reverse Image Search to check for reposted images

If a Friend or Child is Targeted

✓ **DO:**
- **Stay calm** and **nonjudgmental**
- Reassure them that they're not to blame
- Help gather evidence and report it
- Encourage them to take back control by blocking and getting help

✗ **DON'T:**
- Panic, blame, or demand to know "why they sent something"
- Try to handle it alone if the victim is underage - involve appropriate authorities
- Share the image or info with others unnecessarily

Sextortion Is Increasing - But So Is Awareness

Here are some recent statistics gathered from various online sources:

- In 2023, the FBI received over **20,000 reports** of sextortion targeting minors alone.

- Most victims are aged **14 to 30**, but cases exist in every age bracket.

- The rise of **AI deepfake tech** means even those who never shared explicit images are now targets

The good news? **Awareness works**. More people are speaking out. Platforms and law enforcement are catching up. The silence that scammers count on is starting to break.

A Real-Life Example

Not too long ago I was asked by a friend if I could help her son. He had been taken-in by a young woman who had convinced him to send her some intimate images. But it wasn't a young girl, it was a scammer - **it was a typical case of sextortion**. The scammer wanted money otherwise they were going to send the images to his contacts, friends and family.

In a panic, before he realised that the best thing to do was to tell his mother, he sent the scammer two payments via PayPal totalling almost $800 (US) and **the scammer was continuing to ask for even more money**.

Using the screenshots, email and other evidence that he had gathered, **I was able to trace the scammer back to the Philippines**. Armed with their phone number, email address, location and even the make and model of their phone, **I confronted the scammer** - they were shocked to have been identified so easily - and, fearing being arrested, **they agreed to delete the photos and to leave him alone**.

That was three years ago, **the photos were never sent to anyone and he hasn't heard from the scammer since**.

This case had a very positive result, mostly I believe, because the scammer was acting alone. Many sextortion cases however, are linked to large organised groups, such as the **Yahoo Boys whose core members are based in Nigeria**. If my friend's son had been taken-in by one of these large groups then I am quite certain that they would not have backed-down so easily when confronted.

A Few Things Perhaps I Shouldn't Say

There will be mixed views on what I am about to say - particularly from those people who say to *never* send intimate photos to anyone - but if you are an adult then ultimately it is your choice whether you are going to "send nudes" and accept the possible risk of sextortion and humiliation.

If you are not yet an adult (i.e. under 16, or under 18 in some cases) then *never under any circumstances send intimate photos to anyone* - bear in mind that often, scammers and child sex offenders will pose as another child, and start by asking you for a photo of you in your swimsuit or underwear - and if you send that, they will then use that photo to blackmail you into sending them something much more intimate and revealing. Block and report anyone straight away that asks you to do this.

Let's assume you are an adult and you have read this book, and despite the warnings, you are still wanting to send intimate photos to somebody that you only know through online contact.

Firstly, have you already checked their identity with reverse image searches and by using facial recognition? (see chapter 15). Are you sure you are talking to someone who is really who they say they are? What do the search results tell you? Is it the face of someone whose photos are widely available online - like a model, celeb or adult actor?

If you do choose to go ahead, then consider keeping your face out of the photos and having a plain background - both of these make it hard for a scammer to blackmail you as you can't be identified in the photos.

Maybe ask them to go first instead, and see what you get sent - probably something they downloaded from the Internet?

Remember...
　　If you get taken-in by a scammer, you made a mistake - you trusted someone. You were manipulated. That's not a crime - **but what they are doing is.**

Shame only sticks if you let it. But once you talk about it, report it, and reclaim control - their power vanishes.

Believe me when I say your family and friends would much rather you tell them right away if this should happen to you - don't keep it to yourself and don't let it take over. You don't have to go through it alone. And you don't have to give in.

"There's no shame in being tricked. The shame belongs to the blackmailer."

Help is out there. Use it.

CHAPTER FOURTEEN

Spotting Online Impersonation & Deepfakes - Trust, But Verify

"You can't believe everything you see online anymore - even if it's a video of someone or something."

In an age where technology can mimic your face, your voice, and even your writing style, trust is becoming one of the most manipulated commodities online. Deepfakes, impersonation scams, and synthetic media are changing how we perceive truth - and how scammers exploit it.

This chapter will help you:
- Understand what deepfakes and impersonation scams are
- Identify the signs of fake audio, video, and profiles
- Recognise how these tools are weaponised for fraud, manipulation, and blackmail
- Learn how to verify digital content before reacting or sharing
- Arm yourself with tools and strategies to stay ahead

What Is Online Impersonation?

Different to social media impersonation which we have already discussed - this chapter takes a look at the types of deep-fakes and AI often used by criminals - such as images, video, voices, or full profiles to deceive others.

Common forms include:
- Spoofed email or text messages
- AI-generated voices (e.g., a "CEO" calling for an urgent money transfer)
- Deepfaked AI videos of politicians, celebrities or loved ones

Why it matters: Impersonation is used to commit fraud, disinformation, harassment, and social engineering.

What Are Deepfakes?

The term "Deepfake" was coined in 2017 by a moderator on the Reddit platform - it was also his username or "handle" at the time. It combined a term taken from a branch of AI that used neural networks, called "Deep Learning", and unsurprisingly, the word "fake".

It is synthetic media generated using AI - most commonly:
- Video: Making someone appear to say or do something they didn't
- Images: Creating realistic photos of people, some of who don't exist
- Audio: Mimicking a person's voice
- Text: Social media posts pretending to be written by someone else

Commercially, very few online AI sites allow this type of deceptive use, some AI sites will outright refuse to manipulate images of someone else. However, anyone with a bit of technical know how can build their own AI model at home, simply by downloading any one of a variety of online frameworks and training it on specific data. Worryingly, this allows criminals to create their own disturbingly convincing fakes - cheaply and quickly - and without any regulation.

If you want to see for yourself how good AI has become at generating realistic videos, take a moment to look online at a website called lovegpt.com which generates fake boyfriends and girlfriends. Or try out Google's Gemini AI - their extremely good video creation tool is called Veo.

Real-World Examples

CEO Fraud Using AI Voice Cloning
A finance employee received a call that sounded exactly like their company's CEO, instructing them to urgently transfer $240,000. The voice was an AI clone.

Deepfake Politician Video

In 2022, a fake video of a world leader saying they were surrendering to a rival nation spread on social media, briefly causing panic and confusion before being debunked.

Romance Scam with AI-Generated Faces or Video

Instead of stealing people's online photos, scammers are now using AI generated, photorealistic images and video of attractive people to lure victims on dating sites, request money, or gain sensitive information.

How to Spot Deepfakes & Impersonation

When it comes to images and video, keep these tell-tale clues in mind as they will help you spot some of the fakes. But bear in mind that as the quality of AI improves, the visual clues will become harder to spot. Here are some of the easiest cues to spot:

✗ *Unnatural blinking or facial expressions* - Deepfakes often get eye movement wrong

✗ *Flickering or inconsistent lighting* - Look for weird shadows or transitions

✗ *Lip sync doesn't match speech* - Mismatches between audio and video

✗ *Artefacts around the face* - Blurring, jagged edges, or colour distortion

✗ *Poor rendering of ears, teeth, hands* - AI still struggles with some features

✗ *Object or people size and scale* - Does everything seem in proportion?

Some Examples of Tools to Use:
The above list should be sufficient in helping you detect a fake, but if you want a second-opinion or to try something a bit more technical, then tools will be of interest:

- InVID browser plugin for video verification
- Deepware Scanner - detects deepfakes
- Hive Moderation - fake image detection
- FotoForensics - image metadata & error level analysis

For Social Media & Profiles
If you use social media frequently then you may already be accustomed to recognising these tell-tale signs of fake accounts:

✗ *Generic or misspelled usernames* - like michaelj0rdan_real or ceo_karen_new

✗ *Profile photo looks too perfect* - may be AI-generated or stolen

✗ *Low activity or engagement* - few posts, no mutual friends, weird follower/following ratio

✗ *Recent account creation* - scammers often make new profiles for each scam run

✗ *Urgent or emotional messages* - asking for money, help, or secrets quickly

How many times have you followed a celebrity, a financial advisor or a crypto investor only to have random cloned accounts start following and messaging you, pretending to be that person's "other, secret account" or an "account just for their most special fans" ? By now you know where this is going... They are scammers after your money - most commonly they will start to DM you and talk about their "amazing crypto investment opportunity" and then ask you to invest in it.

A Real Life Example

A few years ago we were contacted by someone who for over 5 years had been sending money to cover fees in relation to precious stones and metals that she was offered a share of (a fairly common precious metals scam) - sending over £200,000 in total.

She had jumped at the chance to get involved because her favourite actor had asked her to - "Tom Cruise". Notice I put his name in quotes, because quite obviously it had nothing to do with the real Tom Cruise - it was a scammer impersonating him, who had drawn her in to his far-fetched scam by using emotion and urgency.

The scammer had seen online that she was "Tom Cruise's biggest fan", he used that to convince her that he was the real Tom Cruise and that he was messaging from his "personal social media account". The scammer used Tom Cruise's full name - Thomas Cruise Mapother IV - which in itself should be a red flag, as scammers often include too much detail, such as full names, thinking that doing so will make them more credible.

Pro Tips:
- Reverse-image search the profile photo (e.g., Google Images, Yandex or PimEyes)
- Check if the person already has a verified account elsewhere
- Ask mutual friends about any "odd" messages

Where Impersonation Scams Happen

Impersonal scams come in all shapes and sizes, and the methods change on a regular basis. Here are a few examples of how you may be approached:

Email - Spoofed domain names, fake HR requests, the "boss" money transfer requests

LinkedIn - Fake recruiter profiles phishing for resumes or personal info

Facebook / Instagram / X - Fake celeb giveaways or investment opportunities

WhatsApp / Texts - "Hi Mom, I changed my number. Can you send money?"

Video calls - AI avatars or voice deepfakes in real time (rare, but rising)

If someone suddenly messages you with an urgent request - **verify it through a second channel** before acting.

How to Verify Suspicious Content

Here's a simple checklist to verify questionable media:

✓ **Step-by-Step Verification:**
1. **Ask yourself**: Is this emotionally manipulative, urgent or too sensational?
2. **Check the source**: Is it a credible news outlet or random TikTok?
3. **Use reverse search**: Look up images, quotes, or video stills
4. **Search the transcript**: Has it been fact-checked

already?
5. **Check metadata (EXIF)**: Tools like FotoForensics can reveal tampering
6. **Cross-check with official sources**: Companies, celebrity agents, or authorities.

Some Examples of Tools to Use:
- Yandex or Google Reverse Image Search
- InVID (video frame analysis)
- Sensity AI (deepfake detection for enterprise)
- Fact-checking sites like Snopes, PolitiFact, Reuters Fact Check

A Worrying AI Development

Recently there was **a proof-of-concept video** circulating on LinkedIn, demonstrating how a scammer could make a fake AI video call to an unsuspecting victim by passing the call through his laptop - and **his laptop replaced his face and voice, in real-time**, with the face and voice of the person the scammer was impersonating.

The real-time aspect of this is very worrying, because **the video moved and spoke when the scammer did**. It also mapped his facial expressions on to the AI version. It looked and sounded just like the person he was impersonating. In this proof-of-concept version, there was a very slight look of AI generation, but I have no doubt that will be ironed out in the near future.

So, if a scammer is able to realistically change their face and voice in real-time on a video call, future impersonation scams will be extremely difficult to spot.

How to Protect Yourself from Being Impersonated

Ask yourself what somebody impersonating you would be doing? Searching your name online and reverse image searching your profile photo/s is a good way to find out if anyone is impersonating you.

- **Keep your personal content private** - Limit what's publicly available about you, especially voice recordings and high-res face shots.
- **Use unique profile photos** - Avoid stock-like images that can be cloned or stolen.
- **Google yourself regularly** - Check for impersonation accounts using your name, photos, or likeness.
- **Report fakes immediately** - All major platforms allow impersonation reporting. Enlist friends to help report faster.
- **Use account verification and two-factor authentication** - This won't prevent clones but can protect your original profile from takeover.
- **Be careful what you share in video and voice chats** - Audio samples can be used for voice cloning.

Set Up Codewords and Passphrases

Perhaps the best way to protect ourselves against modern impersonation scams, whether a text message, voice or video call, is to have a pre-agreed codeword or passphrase in place with family and coworkers. If the AI proof-of-concept video that I mentioned above starts to get used by scammers, then using codewords may be the only way to stop a scammer in their tracks.

Example 1: A scammer impersonating a company CEO calls his accounts team and asks them to make a large payment. But the scammer doesn't know that the company has a codeword in place. The attempted fraud fails.

Example 2: A parent receives a text from a scammer "Hi mum, I've lost my phone and purse, this is my new number. Can you send me £100?" the parent asks for the agreed word or phrase. The attempted fraud fails.

Can AI Help Detect Deepfakes?

Yes, but it's a cat-and-mouse game. Many tools and platforms use AI to detect deepfakes, but scammers are constantly improving their techniques. As detection improves, so does deception.

That's why **human awareness is still your best defence**.

Does AI Have Positive Uses?

Yes, of course, far too many positive uses to mention here. AI is a great efficiency tool, greatly speeding up tasks for businesses and has multiple uses in the medical community.

I actually used ChatGPT to generate all of the images in this book, as well as to make the image for the front cover - doing so saved me a huge amount of time.

Beware though, AI does make mistakes, those mistakes are called 'hallucinations', and because of that you should always manually check anything that AI has done for you.

Summary

Deepfakes and impersonation attacks are no longer science fiction. They're here - and they're getting better every day. But with a sceptical mindset, the right tools, and a healthy habit of double-checking before believing, you can spot the fakes and avoid falling for them.

Key Takeaways:
- Impersonation can happen via voice, video, email, or text
- **Deepfakes are improving fast** - watch for inconsistencies and emotional manipulation
- Verify before you trust - especially if money, urgency, or secrecy is involved
- Protect your own identity by limiting what you share online

In a world where reality can be faked, critical thinking becomes your best protection.

CHAPTER FIFTEEN
The Power of Reverse Image Search - Unmasking Fake Profiles

"If a scammer stole someone's face to build their lie, a reverse image search helps you find the truth."

Scammers often hide behind **fake identities**, using stolen or AI-generated photos to gain your trust. That attractive military officer? The successful entrepreneur? The person who looks like a model that just stepped out of a catalog?

Chances are, that photo came from **someone else's real life** - and that person has no idea they're being impersonated.

That's where **reverse image search** comes in.

In this chapter, you'll learn exactly how to use it - and how to spot signs that a profile is a fake.

What Is Reverse Image Search?
Reverse image search lets you upload or paste the URL of a photo - and then search the internet for **other places where that photo appears.**

It's the digital equivalent of saying *"Where else has this photo or face been used online?"*

It's incredibly useful for:
- Detecting **stolen photos**
- Unmasking **fake dating or social media profiles**
- Identifying **AI-generated or celebrity images**
- Seeing if someone is lying about who they are

Tools You Can Use

Here are the top tools that I use for reverse image searching:

1. Google Images
- https://images.google.com
- Works well for finding where a photo appears across websites, news articles, and profiles. Google is no longer useful for facial searches, but is good for tracing the entire photograph or just an object that appears in the photograph.

2. TinEye
- https://tineye.com
- Great for detecting **exact matches** of a photo, even if it's been resized or slightly edited

3. Yandex Images
- https://yandex.com/images/
- Russia-based search engine with **strong facial matching**
- Good at finding similar-looking people or the same face in different poses
- Finds matches that other tools sometimes miss

4. PimEyes (best paid option for faces)
- https://pimeyes.com
- Powerful tool for identifying faces - often used by journalists and investigators
- Pro Tip: you can run the search without paying and get an good idea based on the preview of the results. You can still pay if you wish to fully unlock the results.

Step-by-Step: Reverse Searching a Suspected Scammer
Here's how to do it using **Google Images** and **Yandex**:

Method 1: Google Reverse Image Search

Option A: Using a photo you downloaded or a screenshot
1. Go to images.google.com
2. Click the **camera icon** in the search bar
3. Select **"Upload a file"**
4. Upload the suspect photo
5. Adjust the 4-white corners so that the whole image is selected
6. To identify just a part of the photo then adjust the 4-white corners accordingly

Option B: Using a photo from a website or profile
1. Right-click the photo
2. Choose **"Copy image address"**
3. Paste the link into Google Images using the **camera icon**
4. Adjust the 4-white corners so that the whole image is selected

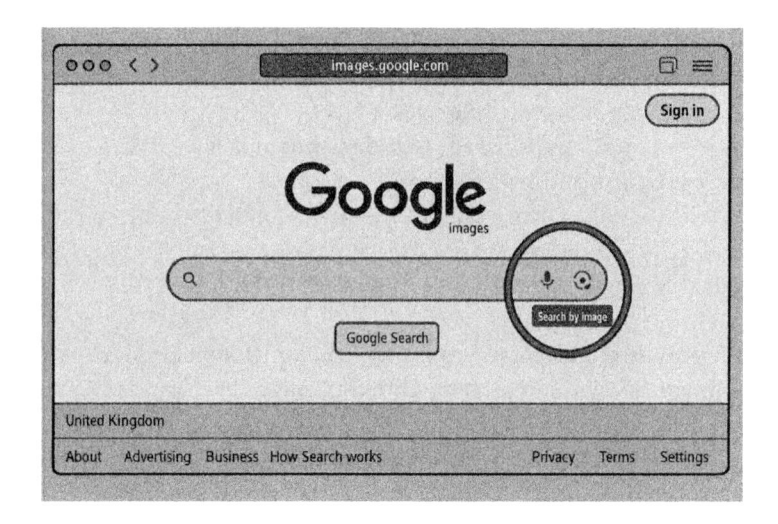

Google will show you:
- Websites where the photo has appeared
- Similar images or variations of the image
- News articles or social profiles using the same image

What to look for:
- Is the same image linked to a **different name** or profile?
- Is it from a **modelling website, celebrity page, or stock photo site**?
- Are there many identical images but with different backstories?

Pro Tip: In recent years, Google has removed the facial recognition feature from their searches, instead designing the service to focus more on objects (I assume for online shopping purposes?) but this can still be useful if you want to search for an object or feature in a photo.

Method 2: Yandex

Yandex is currently a better choice than Google for this
1. Go to https://yandex.com/images
2. Click the **camera icon** next to the search bar
3. Upload the photo or paste a link
4. Yandex will show:
    - Other versions of the photo
    - Websites using it
    - Similar faces (sometimes in different poses or with different clothes)

Yandex is especially good at:
- Finding photos that have been **slightly altered**
- Detecting **AI or deepfake composites** (by showing close matches)
- Identifying the **real person** in the image

I have detailed instructions on my website realorcatfish.com which take you through step-by-step from saving or screenshotting their images through how to carry out the various types of reverse image search.

Red Flags to Watch For

If any of the following show up during your search, it's a major warning sign:

✗ **The same photo belongs to:**
- A **celebrity or influencer**
- A completely different person (different name, different story)
- A **military or model stock photo**
- A **news article about romance scams** or identity theft

✗ **No results at all**
- Could mean it is an **AI-generated image**
- Or a photo that's never been used online before (rare for genuine profiles)
- Use sites like thispersondoesnotexist.com to compare against AI faces

Additional Tools for Deeper Investigations
EXIF Metadata Viewers
- Can show when/where a photo was taken (if not stripped out by social media)
- Try uploading the image to this website to view the data: jimpl.com

Deepfake Detection
- AI tools like HuggingFace - deepfake detectors can sometimes help

- Look for strange backgrounds, inconsistent lighting, or odd reflections in the eyes

What To Do If You Discover a Fake Profile
Step 1: Don't Confront the Scammer
- They may become aggressive or simply vanish
- You can't "shame" someone who's already criminal

Step 2: Report the Profile
- On Instagram, Facebook, or dating sites: use "Report" - "Fake account" or "Impersonation"
- Include the results of your reverse image search if you can.

Step 3: Warn Others (if safe to do so)
- If you were initially contacted by the scammer, they may be targeting others too
- On dating apps, consider reporting via the app's support channel

Real Example: "It Was a Model's Photo from 2012"
"He said he was a deployed soldier. But the photo came up on a blog from 2012 - the same face, same uniform. Turns out, the scammer was using the identity of a real man who died overseas. I reported it and blocked him. Reverse image search saved me."

Reverse Search Your Own Photos
If you have ever been approached by a scammer, it is a good idea to reverse search your own profile images to see if the scammer has copied them and is using them as part of another scam. If you use just one or two profile photos then a Yandex or TinEye search may be sufficient, but if you change

your profile photos frequently than a facial recognition search, such as PimEyes, will be better as it looks for your face rather than a matching photo.

Reverse Image Search Is a Scam-Busting Superpower

It's fast. It's often free. And it's one of the most powerful tools for spotting lies before they turn into heartbreak or financial ruin.

If something feels off, trust your instincts - and search the photo.

CHAPTER SIXTEEN
The Dark Web - What It Is, and Why It Matters

"The Dark Web isn't all evil - but it's where a lot of evil hides."

The phrase "Dark Web" sounds dramatic - like something out of a spy movie or a hacker thriller. And while it does have a shadowy reputation, it's important to separate **fact from fear**.

This chapter explains what the Dark Web really is, how it works, what's legal (and not), and how it plays a central role in online crime - from stolen data to drug deals to digital hitmen. But we'll also look at its legitimate uses - because yes, those exist too.

Whether you're just curious or trying to understand how stolen information is sold, this chapter will shine a light into the shadows.

What Is the Dark Web?

At its core, the dark web is **a part of the internet that isn't indexed by standard search engines** like Google, Yahoo or Bing.

You can't just type an ".onion" site address into your normal web browser and expect it to load. To access the dark web, you need special software - most commonly people use the **Tor browser**, which routes your traffic through a network of encrypted relay nodes.

The Internet Can be Described as Having 3 Layers:

It all runs on the same infrastructure, but it varies on whether we can see it openly or not. The Internet is best described as having 3 layers:

Surface Web - The World Wide Web - sites you can find on a search engine, such as Google - such as news pages, websites, Wikipedia and YouTube.

Deep Web - Password-protected content not usually indexed by search engines - such as email accounts and private databases

Dark Web - Hidden sites accessible only with tools like the Tor browser, and not visible to regular browsers

So the **Dark Web** isn't technically "hidden", **it's just inaccessible without the right tools**. It is also hard to search, so it is quite difficult to find things on there.

Is It Legal to Use?

Surprisingly to many: **Yes, the Dark Web is legal to access.**

Using tools like the Tor browser is 100% legal in most countries, including the U.S., UK, Australia, Canada, and EU nations. In fact, journalists, activists, and even law enforcement agencies use it.

However - and this is critical - **what you do on the Dark Web** may be very illegal.

I recall two occasions, once at the **ITV television studios** and once at the offices of the **Mirror newspaper**, where their IT departments **wouldn't let me use their network** to connect to the Dark Web for features we were working on - I had to use my phone as a hotspot for my laptop. On those occasions that was probably the right thing to do, as we were researching some of the darkest corners of the Dark Web.

Legal uses:
- Anonymous communication for whistleblowers
- Accessing censored content in authoritarian countries
- Research, journalism, privacy testing
- Having a casual look to see what it's about

Illegal uses:
- Buying/selling drugs, weapons, or hacked data
- Hiring a hitman or a hacker
- Sharing exploitative content
- Selling stolen identities or ransomware kits

The **tool is legal** but **it is the intent which matters**.

How Does It Work?

The Tor Network:

Tor (short for "The Onion Router") bounces your traffic through multiple servers (nodes) around the world, peeling a layer of encryption off it each time - like layers of an onion. The path your traffic takes through the network changes every few minutes to make it difficult to monitor. In addition, each of the nodes your traffic flows through only knows about the next node in your path - no single node knows about the whole route, making it very hard to locate you and identify what you are doing.

• Your ISP can see that you are using Tor, but not what you're doing

• The website you visit doesn't know your real IP address

• This creates anonymity - or at least, the appearance of it

.onion Websites
Dark web URL's end in ".onion" and the newer Version 3 addresses are 56-characters in length, these sites can only be accessed using a special browser, such as the Tor browser.

This is a representative example of an .onion URL:
http://duskhtlmq9pxv4wz1no5ry3bj6se8iu0af4dc.onion

These URLs use long, randomised strings to make them hard to remember and harder to detect, and some URL's do change from time to time.

The Good Side of the Dark Web
Believe it or not, the dark web isn't entirely criminal. There are legitimate and even noble uses, including:

Privacy and Freedom of Speech
• Journalists in oppressive regimes use the dark web to communicate and publish safely
• Human rights groups host anonymous tip lines
• Whistleblowers like Edward Snowden used Tor to share sensitive info

Censorship Resistance
• Citizens in countries with internet censorship (like China or Iran) use the dark web to access blocked news and information

Security Research
• Ethical hackers and academics study malware, underground markets, and vulnerabilities for public good

The Dark Side: Crime and Commerce

Unfortunately, the dark web is also **a massive underground marketplace** for illegal goods and services.

Popular criminal activities include:

Data theft - Sale of stolen credit cards, logins, full identity profiles ("Fullz")

Drugs - Marketplaces for everything from weed to fentanyl to LSD

Weapons - Some sellers offer guns, explosives, or even "clean" serials

Ransomware-as-a-Service (RaaS) - Rentable tools to attack organisations for profit

Hacked accounts - Netflix, Uber, PayPal, banking credentials

Child exploitation material - Tragically, still a persistent issue despite takedown efforts

Fake documents - Passports, diplomas, vaccination cards, driver's licenses

These markets often look surprisingly professional, with:
- Product descriptions
- Seller reviews
- Escrow payment systems (often in **cryptocurrency** like Monero or Bitcoin)
- Customer support

Examples of infamous marketplaces:
- **Silk Road** - The original dark web drug market (shut down in 2013)
  - **AlphaBay** - Became even larger, taken down in 2017
  - **Hydra** - Russian-language market, shut down in 2022
  - New marketplaces constantly pop up to replace ones

taken down

Is It Really Anonymous?
Not entirely. **Tor is private, but not bulletproof.**

Your identity can still be exposed through:
- Malware that reveals your IP address or location
- JavaScript exploits in your browser
- Logging into real accounts through the Dark Web (email, Facebook, etc.)
- Leaking metadata (time zones, language settings, screen resolution)
- Law enforcement surveillance - yes, this happens a lot

Big takeaways:
- Tor anonymises your traffic - not your behaviour
- Mistakes can unmask you
- Law enforcement regularly infiltrate dark web sites

Why It Matters for You
You may never use the dark web, but it still can affect you.

Remember that leaked password from the Netflix phishing email? It might be up for sale on a dark web forum right now. That stolen identity? Sold to a scammer building a new romance profile. That ransomware attack you read about in the news? It probably started with someone buying malware-as-a-service on the dark web.

So why does this matter?
- Awareness equals Preparedness
- If you understand how stolen data is used, you'll be more motivated to protect it
- The dark web shows just how valuable your digital

identity really is

How to Check if Your Data Is on the Dark Web

You can't browse dark web markets yourself easily - but I would advise that you shouldn't, unless you're an IT whizz, or else you may find you accidentally end up on a list at Interpol. However, you can use legitimate services to see if your info has been leaked:

Example Tools:
- haveibeenpwned.com - Checks if your email appears in known breaches
- Credit monitoring services (such as Experian, Equifax and Credit Karma)
- Identity theft protection plans CIFAS (UK) Norton, Aura, LifeLock, etc

If your data shows up as having been leaked, change your passwords immediately and enable 2FA everywhere.

Telegram Messenger

Criminal activity and child sexual abuse material (CSAM) on the Dark Web was at a peak roughly around 2012 - after which, due to better policing and detection methods, criminals started to look elsewhere. Crime and CSAM are still very much present on the Dark Web, but people are "less-trusting" of Dark Web marketplaces nowadays, because law enforcement agencies are known to take over the sites and continue running them in order to identify and arrest active users.

Instead, criminals have been moving to end-to-end encrypted messaging apps - with Telegram being one of the more popular choices. You may remember in August 2024 that

Telegram's owner, Pavel Durov, was arrested in France, for failing to properly moderate the amount of illegal activity on the app. Speaking publicly after his arrest, Durov indicated that he would introduce moderation tools in to Telegram.

Summary

The dark web is a hidden part of the internet - not inherently evil, but home to a wide array of illegal marketplaces and communities.

Key Takeaways:

• Accessing the dark web is legal, but many activities on it are not

• It requires special tools to access it, like the Tor browser

• It's used for both privacy reasons and for criminal activity

• Most online scams, stolen data, and ransomware tools pass through the dark web

• Anonymity is never guaranteed

You don't need to visit the dark web to be affected by it. But understanding it helps you defend yourself.

CHAPTER SEVENTEEN

What to Do If You're Scammed - Recovery & Damage Control

"What you do next is what matters most."

Despite our best efforts, anyone can fall victim to a scam. The important thing is to act quickly, minimise damage, and learn how to bounce back stronger. Whether it was a phishing attack, fake tech support, a romance scam, or identity theft, there are always steps you can take to regain control.

In this chapter, we'll cover:
- The first steps to take immediately after a scam
- How to report fraud and secure your accounts
- Tools for identity theft recovery
- Emotional recovery and talking to others
- How to make sure it never happens again

Step 1: Don't Panic - Take Control

Scammers rely on **shame and fear** to keep you silent and passive. But the sooner you act, the more you can recover.

If you realise you've:

- Clicked a suspicious link
- Given away sensitive info (password, credit card details, etc)
- Sent money or crypto to a scammer
- Installed suspicious software

...then your mission is to **contain the damage and report it.**

Step 2: Secure Your Accounts

If your password or login credentials were exposed, act immediately.

Priority checklist:

1. **Change your password** on the affected account(s)
- Use a **new, strong, unique** password
- If you used that password anywhere else, change it there too

2. **Enable two-factor authentication (2FA)** on all important accounts

3. **Check for unauthorised activity**
- Look at recent logins, purchases, messages sent, changes made

4. **Log out of other sessions**
- Most major platforms such as Google, Facebook, Amazon, etc. will let you force-logout all other devices currently logged in to your account

5. **Run a malware scan**
- Use a trusted tool like Malwarebytes or Bitdefender to scan for keyloggers or spyware

Step 3: Financial Protection

If you shared banking, credit card, debit card, or PayPal details:

Call your bank immediately:
- **Freeze or cancel** the card - many banking apps let you freeze your own card
- **Dispute charges** as being fraudulent
- **Request a new card** or account number if necessary

For PayPal, Venmo, Zelle, etc.:
- File a fraud report through their app or website
- Request a refund
- If sent to a scammer's email or username, **screenshot everything** for your report

For crypto transactions:
- Unfortunately, most crypto transactions are irreversible
- Report to the relevant exchange (Coinbase, Binance, etc.)
- Document the wallet address(es) used in the scam
- Report the scam to local law enforcement

Step 4: Report the Scam

Reporting helps authorities track patterns, shut down fake websites, and protect others. Many reporting organisations are US-centric, however if you search online you will find that most countries will have their own alternative.

Examples of types of scam and where to report them:

General fraud (UK) - actionfraud.org.uk
General fraud (US) - reportfraud.ftc.gov
General Fraud (Canada) - antifraudcentre-centreantifraude.ca
Phishing emails - Forward to reportphishing@apwg.org
Identity theft - identitytheft.gov
Romance scams - IC3.gov and dating app support

Social media fraud - Report via the social media platform

You can also do the following:
- File a local police report (especially if large amounts or identity theft)
- Contact your country's consumer protection agency

Step 5: Identity Theft Response
If the scam involved personal information like:
- Driver's license or passport
- Address, bank account or card details
- Your Social Security Number (US) or medical records

Then stay alert and be prepared to take action on any long-term fraud attempts.

In addition, **U.S. Residents** can:

1. **Visit** identitytheft.gov
   - Create a recovery plan
   - File a report with the FTC

2. **Contact credit bureaus** (Equifax, Experian and TransUnion)
   - Request a **fraud alert** or **credit freeze**

3. **Check your credit report** for unusual activity

4. **Notify the IRS** if your SSN was exposed: irs.gov/identity-theft

Step 6: Emotional Recovery
Many victims feel embarrassed, ashamed, or angry - especially after romance scams, impersonation fraud, or investment schemes.

But remember:
- **Scammers are well rehearsed professionals**, and you are

not to blame
- You're **not alone** - millions fall victim every year
- Talking about it helps others avoid similar traps

Consider:
- Speaking with a friend (or therapist)
- Joining online support groups (Reddit's r/scams, orScamWatch groups)
- Would you share your story anonymously online to help educate others?

Step 7: Lock Down Your Digital Life

Once the immediate crisis is under control, it's time to build stronger defences:

✓ Password Hygiene
- Change all major account passwords
- Use a password manager to securely store your passwords

✓ Secure Devices
- Scan your devices for malware
- Remove unknown apps and browser extensions
- Check if your browser's start page or search page has been changed

✓ Stop any Phishing Vectors
- Report scam emails as spam or mark them as junk mail
- Don't respond to any follow-up messages from the scammers
- Unlink compromised phone numbers or email addresses from important accounts

✓ Monitor for Any Reuse of Your Data - Use Services Like:

- HaveIBeenPwned.com to check if your email address has been leaked
- Firefox Monitor - monitor.mozilla.org
- Credit report monitoring tools (Equifax, Experian, Credit Karma, etc)

Some Positive Action in the UK

If you transferred money to a scammer from your UK bank account then there are regulations in place that help protect you and your money:

APP (Authorised Push Payment) Fraud Reimbursement Policy:

- Since October 2024, UK banks and building societies are **required to repay your losses, up to £80,000**
- Known as APP Fraud (**Authorised Push Payment**), it is when you have been tricked into sending a payment to a scammer from your bank or building society account.
- Your losses should be **repaid within 5 business days by the bank** (or within 35 days if there are some issues your bank needs to investigate)
- If your losses are higher than £80,000, or the bank hasn't helped you, then you may have to go to the Financial Ombudsman, who have an upper limit on **compensation of £430,000**
- Your claim to your bank or building society **must be made within 13 months** of the last APP payment that you sent to the scammer.

Real-Life Example: A Scam Recovery Timeline

Day 1:
- John gets a phishing email that looks like PayPal. He enters his login info.
- He realises it was a scam a few hours later.

- He changes his PayPal password, enables 2FA, and checks for recent transactions.
- He contacts PayPal and reports the incident.
- His account is temporarily frozen and secured.
- He uses HaveIBeenPwned to check if his email was in any data breaches.

Day 2:
- John installs a password manager.
- He changes passwords on other accounts that used the same one.
- He starts reading more about digital hygiene.
- John reports the scam to Action Fraud (UK) or the FTC (US).
- He shares his experience on Reddit to help others avoid the same trap.

What to Learn from a Scam

The worst thing you can do is ignore it and hope it never happens again.

Instead:

- Why not see it as a wake-up call to build a safer digital routine
- Teach others around you (especially family members and the elderly)
- Accept that you were a victim of deception, not a failure of intelligence

Summary

Being scammed isn't the end - it's the beginning of smarter digital habits. Quick, clear-headed action can stop the damage and even help others.

Key Takeaways:
• Don't panic. Move quickly to secure accounts and report the scam.
• Contact your bank and credit bureaus if financial info was exposed.
• Use government sites (actionfraud.org.uk, identitytheft.gov, etc) to get help.
• Recover emotionally - don't suffer in silence.
• Fortify your online life going forward with better hygiene and habits.

Every breach is an opportunity to build better defences.

CHAPTER EIGHTEEN
Digital Hygiene - Habits of Highly Secure People

"You don't need to be a security genius to stay secure online."

Just like personal hygiene keeps your body healthy, **digital hygiene** keeps your online life secure. It's about creating habits - small daily, weekly, and monthly actions - that reduce risk, prevent breaches, and protect your identity, privacy, and devices.

In this chapter, we'll explore:
- The core components of digital hygiene
- A checklist of essential security practices
- How to simplify security without making life annoying
- Tips for individuals, families, and small business owners
- How to make security a lifestyle, not a chore

What Is Digital Hygiene?

Digital hygiene refers to the regular practices that keep your online world clean, safe, and organised.

It includes:
- Managing your passwords

- Keeping your software up to date
- Checking your devices and accounts for strange activity
- Controlling how your data is shared
- Staying aware of scams, phishing, and evolving threats

Small, consistent habits prevent big problems later.

Core Pillars of Digital Hygiene

1. Password Hygiene
- Use a unique password for every site
- Store them in a password manager (like 1Password, Bitwarden, or NordPass)
- Use strong passwords (e.g., complex phrases of 4 or more words)
- Never reuse credentials across services and websites

Many tech websites and IT professionals will tell you to change your passwords every 6–12 months, but that isn't necessarily the best solution - the current advice from the NCSC (UK) and NIST (US) is to use complex phrases and ONLY change your password if you know, or suspect, that your accounts or credentials have been compromised.

A complex phrase consists of 4 or more words totalling at least 15-characters in length. They must be random words and not a well known phrase or song lyrics.

Pro Tip: If a site offers 2FA (two-factor authentication), always enable it.

2. Device & App Updates
Software updates aren't just for new features - they often fix serious vulnerabilities.

✓ Check and if not already turned on, set automatic updates for:
  • Operating systems (Windows, macOS, iOS, Android)
  • Browsers (Chrome, Firefox, Safari)
  • Apps - especially messaging, banking, and work-related tools

Don't ignore update prompts. Many major hacks could have been prevented with an update (patch) that already existed. The UK's National Cyber Security Centre guidelines stipulate that updates must be installed within 2-weeks of their release.

3. Browser & Online Behaviour

Most attacks today start in your web browser or email inbox.

✓ Best practices:
  • Use a privacy-focused browser (like Firefox, Brave or Safari)
  • Avoid clicking unknown links, especially in emails or pop-ups
  • Never download "free" software from shady sites
  • Use an ad-blocker to reduce exposure to malicious adverts
  • Clear your browser's cookies and cache periodically

4. Account & Identity Management

Your accounts are your attack surface. Keep them lean and locked.

✓ Regular checks:
  • Review account activity (logins, password changes, etc)
  • Remove old apps or accounts you no longer use

- Turn on login alerts (so you get notified when your account is accessed)
- Deactivate or delete unused accounts (they're low-hanging fruit for hackers)

Use the site haveibeenpwned.com to check if your email address and passwords have been exposed in any of the major data breaches.

5. Email Hygiene
Phishing is still the number-one attack method.

✓ Email habits that protect you:
- Don't open attachments from unknown senders
- Hover over links before clicking them - does the URL look legit?
- Use a spam filter and report phishing emails
- Avoid using your main email address for random newsletter subscriptions
- Consider a separate "junk email account" for shopping sites and newsletters

If something looks urgent, emotional, or too good to be true, always assume it is suspicious until proven otherwise.

Weekly & Monthly Digital Hygiene Checklist

Daily - Be mindful of links and apps you engage with
Weekly - Check bank and credit card transactions
Weekly - Review spam folder for any legit emails
Bi-Weekly - Update software, apps and any browser extensions

Monthly - Run a full antivirus/anti-malware scan (e.g., Malwarebytes)

Quarterly - Review privacy settings on social media and apps

Annually - Audit your digital footprint: Google your name, close unused accounts and review permissions

Mobile Hygiene

Smartphones are powerful computers in your pocket and can be just as vulnerable.

✓ Secure your phone:
- Use a strong screen lock code (not just a 4-digit PIN)
- Enable biometric login (Face ID or fingerprint)
- Don't install apps from outside the App Store / Play Store
- Limit app permissions - does that calculator really need to know your location?
- Use "Find My Device" features in case of loss or theft

Tools That Make It Easier

Password Manager (Bitwarden or 1Password) - Stores & autofills strong passwords

2FA App (such as Google Authenticator) - Adds extra security layer to logins

Antivirus (e.g. Malwarebytes, Bitdefender) - Blocks malware, phishing, exploits

Privacy Extension (uBlock Origin, HTTPS Everywhere) - Secures browser traffic

Data Monitor (HaveIBeenPwned, Firefox Monitor) - Alerts you to data breaches

Set them up once and they'll continue to work for you in the background.

Digital Minimalism: Less to Manage equals Less to Hack

Every account, app, and device you use is another potential weakness.

✓ Reduce your digital clutter:
- Close accounts you don't use anymore
- Delete apps that are outdated or suspicious
- Use fewer cloud services, try to use the more trusted ones
- Avoid signing into random sites with your Facebook or Google account

Fewer accounts equals fewer chances of compromise.

Digital Hygiene for Families

Some of these suggestions may be good to implement:
- Set rules for screen time, app installations, and device use
- Use **family accounts** to monitor shared subscriptions and app purchases
- Teach kids and teens about scams, privacy, and digital footprints
- Use routers with built-in parental controls - most routers have built-in parental controls nowadays and some work with the likes of Eero or Netgear Armor, etc.

Digital Hygiene for Small Business Owners

Small businesses are often cybercriminals' favourite targets due to their perceived weaker defences.

✓ Key steps:
 • Back up your data regularly (both in the cloud and offline)
 • Segment Wi-Fi: one for employees, one for guests
 • Train staff on phishing and social engineering awareness
 • Use business-grade antivirus and email protection
 • Have a simple incident response plan (who to call, how to isolate an infected device, what to do next, etc)

Mindset Matters Most

Even with all the tools, your mindset is your best security system.

✓ Think Like a Hacker:
 • How would someone try to trick me?
 • What info could be used against me if stolen?
 • What's the worst that could happen if this account got hacked?

Then act accordingly.

Summary

Security isn't about being perfect. It's about **making yourself a difficult target** by maintaining good digital hygiene.

Key Takeaways:
 • Use strong, unique passwords stored in a password manager
 • Keep your devices and apps updated
 • Be cautious about links, downloads, and unfamiliar messages
 • Audit your accounts, permissions, and privacy settings regularly

- Think critically before clicking, sharing, or trusting

Treat your data like you'd treat your money - because, in many ways, it is.

CHAPTER NINETEEN

Hardening Your Devices - How to Lock Down Your Phone and Computer

"Your devices are your digital life, and right now, your front door might be wide open."

You wouldn't leave your house unlocked with your valuables on display, but many people do just that with their devices.

Your smartphone and computer store your identity, your money, your private conversations, your location, and more. If someone gains access - through malware, phishing, or just bad luck - they could hijack your entire life.

This chapter is a bit technical, but I've tried to keep it simple and walk you through the steps required to tighten the security settings on:
- iPhones
- Android phones
- Windows PCs
- Apple Macs

No need to be an expert - just follow the checklists and if

anything is not clear then look on my Real or Catfish website, realorcatfish.com, for helpful videos and "How To" articles.

iPhone Security (iOS 17 and newer)

Apple's ecosystem is already privacy-focused, but you can - and should - harden it further.

✓ 1. Use a Strong Passcode
- Use 6 digits or longer
- Or even better: Set a custom alphanumeric passcode
- Settings → Face ID & Passcode → Change Passcode → Passcode Options

✓ 2. Enable Face ID & Turn On Attention Detection
- Prevents unlocking when you're not looking
- Settings → Face ID & Passcode → Require Attention for Face ID

✓ 3. Turn on Two-Factor Authentication (2FA) for Apple ID
- Settings → Tap your name → Password & Security → Two-Factor Authentication → ON

✓ 4. Disable Lock Screen Access to Sensitive Info
- Stop notifications from showing when locked
- Settings → Notifications → Show Previews → When Unlocked

Disable access when locked to these items:
- Control Center (prevents phone thieves putting your phone in flight mode)
- Siri
- Wallet
- Reply with Message
- Settings → Face ID & Passcode → "Allow Access When

Locked" → Toggle off

✓ 5. Use App Tracking Transparency
• Stop apps from tracking your behaviour across other apps/sites
• Settings → Privacy & Security → Tracking → Turn off "Allow Apps to Request to Track"

✓ 6. Review App Permissions
• Settings → Privacy & Security
• Go through:
- Location Services → Set to "While Using the App" or "Never"
- Microphone, Camera, Contacts, etc. → Review & limit access

✓ 7. Enable "Find My iPhone" and Activation Lock
• Settings → Your name → Find My → Find My iPhone → ON

✓ 8. Turn Off Auto-Join for Public Wi-Fi
• Settings → Wi-Fi → Auto-Join Hotspot → Ask to Join
• Avoid connecting automatically to unknown networks

✓ 9. Use iCloud Keychain or a Password Manager
• Keeps logins secure without reusing weak passwords

Android Security (Google Pixel / Samsung / Others)
Android varies by brand, but these steps apply to most devices with Android 13 or newer.

✓ 1. Use a Strong Screen Lock
• Settings → Security → Screen Lock → Use a **PIN, password, or pattern**

- Avoid "swipe" or "none"

✓ 2. Enable Biometric Unlock
- Settings → Security → Face Unlock / Fingerprint

✓ 3. Secure Your Google Account with 2FA
- Visit: https://myaccount.google.com/security
- Turn on 2-Step Verification
- Add a backup method (e.g. Authenticator app)

✓ 4. Lock Down App Permissions
- Settings → Privacy or Apps → Permission Manager
- Limit location, camera, mic, contacts, and SMS access

✓ 5. Disable Unknown Sources for App Installs
- Settings → Security → Install Unknown Apps → Only allow trusted apps (e.g. Chrome, Play Store)

✓ 6. Turn On "Find My Device"
- Settings → Security → Find My Device → ON
- Lets you locate, lock, or erase your phone remotely
- Also visit: https://android.com/find

✓ 7. Use Google Play Protect
- Settings → Security → Google Play Protect → Scan device for harmful apps

✓ 8. Review & Remove Unused Apps
- Uninstall apps you no longer use - they may still have permissions and background access

Windows PC (Windows 11 and newer)
Windows PCs are prime targets for viruses, phishing, and ransomware. Here's how to harden them.

✓ 1. Enable BitLocker Drive Encryption
• Settings → Privacy & Security → Device Encryption
(On Pro editions, this may be listed as BitLocker)
Encrypts your hard drive so hackers can't access data if your PC is lost

✓ 2. Turn On Windows Defender (Microsoft Defender)
• Settings → Privacy & Security → Windows Security
Make sure:
- Virus & Threat Protection is ON
- Firewall & Network Protection is ON
- App & Browser Control is enabled (reputation-based protection)

✓ 3. Keep Windows Updated
• Settings → Windows Update → Check for updates
• Enable automatic updates for security patches

✓ 4. Create a Standard (Non-Admin) Daily Use Account
• Settings → Accounts → Other Users → Add someone
• Use a limited user account for day-to-day activities - only use your admin account for installing software

✓ 5. Use a Local or Microsoft Account with 2FA
• https://account.microsoft.com/security
• Turn on two-step verification
- Use an authenticator app or backup codes

✓ 6. Disable Remote Desktop (if unused)
• Settings → System → Remote Desktop → Turn off
- Prevents unauthorised remote access

✓ 7. Uninstall Bloatware & Unused Software

• Settings → Apps → Installed Apps → Remove software you don't use or recognise

✓ 8. Install a Reputable Password Manager
• Bitwarden, 1Password, or LastPass are good options
• Never store passwords in unencrypted Notepad files!

macOS (MacBook / iMac)

Apple Macs are more secure out-of-the-box than Windows, but still need tightening.

✓ 1. Use FileVault Disk Encryption
• System Settings → Privacy & Security → FileVault → Turn On
- Encrypts your entire disk

✓ 2. Enable Firewall
• System Settings → Network → Firewall → Turn On

✓ 3. Keep macOS Updated
• System Settings → General → Software Update → Enable automatic updates

✓ 4. Enable Two-Factor Authentication for Apple ID
• System Settings → Your Apple ID → Password & Security → 2FA → ON

✓ 5. Limit App Permissions
• System Settings → Privacy & Security
• Review permissions for: Camera, Microphone, Location, Files and Folders

✓ 6. Disable Automatic Login
• System Settings → Users & Groups → Login Options →

Require Password Immediately

✓ 7. Use Safari's Privacy Tools
- Safari → Settings → Privacy
  - Block cross-site tracking and prevent fingerprinting
  - Use iCloud Private Relay if available (for IP masking)

✓ 8. Turn Off Bluetooth & AirDrop When Not Needed
- AirDrop → "Contacts Only" or "Receiving Off"
- Bluetooth → Off when not in use

Final Advice: Update, Encrypt, Authenticate

Whether you're using an iPhone, Android, PC or Mac, the three most critical rules are:

✓ 1. Update Regularly
Outdated software is the number 1 way hackers get in. Enable automatic updates and restart often.

✓ 2. Encrypt Your Devices
So even if stolen or hacked, your data is scrambled.

✓ 3. Use Strong Authentication
Biometrics + 2FA + strong passwords = maximum protection.

Need More Help With These Changes?

There are some instructional video guides on my website that will show you how to make these changes. I find that it is much easier to watch somebody demonstrating it to you visually than just reading how to do it in a book

You can't stop every hacker, but you can make your devices tougher to crack.

CHAPTER TWENTY

The Future of Online Scams - AI, Deepfakes & Evolving Threats

"Scammers evolve. So must we."

The cybercrime landscape is changing rapidly. As technology improves, so do the tools available to scammers. Gone are the days of broken-English spam emails alone - today's cybercriminals use AI to write fluent messages, generate deepfake videos, clone voices, and impersonate people with stunning realism.

This chapter explores what's next in online scams - and how to prepare for the wave of digital deception already hitting inboxes, phones, and social media feeds.

What's Changing in the Scam World?

Once again, I find myself coming back to discussing AI - misuse of AI by criminals is by far the greatest threat facing us going forward - cybercrime is no longer the domain of solo hackers in dark basements. It's a booming global **industry**, with:

- Organised scam rings operating like businesses
- Use of AI and automation to increase the scale of their attacks
- Personalised phishing campaigns tailored using your data
- Cheap, easy access to scam tools (a $10 voice clone can fake your boss)
- A growing ecosystem of ransomware-as-a-service and malware kits

To stay ahead, we need to understand where scams are headed.

Bear with me as I go over some points again that we have already discussed - it is important to understand how AI and the ever-changing nature of scams will affect us all going forward. We need to constantly be questioning everything - because scammers will find new, and more believable ways to trick people.

Do you remember in Chapter 14 that I suggested setting up **codewords and passphrases** with family, friends and work colleagues to help identify genuine financial requests? This may well be the best defence for now. Perhaps one day we will all end up having a personal app that generates one-time "family passcodes" - a bit like 2FA.

1. AI-Enhanced Scams

As already discussed, Artificial Intelligence isn't just for good - scammers use it too.

How AI helps scammers:

Text generation - Create realistic emails, love letters, or job offers

Voice cloning - Impersonate someone on a phone call (e.g., your boss)

Image creation - Generate fake profiles or ID documents

Chatbots - Run phishing or romance scams at scale

Deepfake videos - Create fake CEO instructions or blackmail material

Example:
A scammer uses AI to generate a "voice message" from your daughter saying she's been kidnapped and needs ransom money. It sounds real - because it *is* her voice, cloned from public TikTok videos.

Why it works: Your brain recognises the voice. Your emotions kick in before logic can catch up.

2. Deepfakes & Synthetic Media

Deepfakes are AI-generated images, videos, or voices that imitate real people - and they're getting extremely good.

Scam uses include:
- Fake video messages from CEOs ordering money transfers
- Blackmail using fabricated "compromising" videos
- Impersonation of public officials or celebrities
- Fraudulent video job interviews (fake candidate or fake recruiter)

Example:
In 2023, a finance employee was tricked into sending $25,000 after a Zoom call with a "CEO" that turned out to be a deepfaked live-video.

Pro Tip: If something seems rushed or off - ask to move to a verified communications channel or live video call. Don't rely on voice or video alone as proof.

Did I mention that I recommend having a codeword or passphrase to use during these types of conversations about money? If the caller doesn't know, or the message doesn't include the codeword then you should **end the conversation right away**.

3. Advanced Phishing (a.k.a. "Spear Phishing")
Phishing emails used to be easy to spot - misspellings, poor grammar, generic intros.

Now, AI writes perfect messages based on:

- Your name
- Your job

- Your hobbies
- Your recent purchases

This ultra-personalised attack is called **spear phishing**.

Example:
You receive an email from "your manager" referencing a project you worked on - with a Google Docs link that requests your login details. It looks legit. But it's fake.

Pro Tip: Never trust the "from" name on an email. Always check the full email address by clicking on the "from" name (this shows the full email address it came from), and confirm any suspicious requests in person or with a phone call.

4. Impersonation-as-a-Service

Scammers can now **rent** stolen identities, tools, and templates from dark web marketplaces.

Offerings include:
- Fake LinkedIn recruiters
- Full bank login kits
- Fake crypto exchanges
- Cloned websites with matching SSL certificates

Emerging trends:
- Job seekers targeted with fake employment offers
- Professionals tricked by fake "investor interest" emails
- Deepfake conference calls with AI-generated attendees

Pro Tip: If someone is too enthusiastic, too quick to offer money, or too polished - step back. Slow the interaction down and verify independently.

5. Brain Hacking: Manipulating Attention and Emotion

The new wave of scamming isn't just technical, it's psychological.

With AI and behavioural data, scammers can now:
- Time their attacks based on your habits (e.g., when you're stressed or distracted)
- Test multiple messages to see what works on you (A/B testing scams like marketers)
- Use targeted ads to reach you with malicious links

Example:
You see a sponsored ad on Instagram for "The hottest crypto investment of 2025." It leads to a beautiful, functional site. You invest. The site vanishes.

Most countries have laws regulating investment companies and you can look up any companies you see adverts for, to see if they are legitimate or not. In the UK this service is provided by the Financial Conduct Authority - www.fca.org.uk

Pro Tip: Be suspicious of urgency, especially if it's accompanied by praise, flattery, or once-in-a-lifetime promises.

6. Scams Merging with Social Engineering

Many scams in the future will involve a **multi-stage attack**:

1. Initial contact via email or DM
2. Establish trust through long conversations
3. Use AI to fake photos, videos, or references
4. Extract money, data, or favours once trust is built

These scams often play out over **weeks or months**.

Common scam types:
- Romance scams, including "pig butchering scams"
- Hybrid job - where you pay an up front fee, or it can be CV data harvesting
- Crypto or precious metal investments
- Fake scholarship offers
- "Friend in crisis" video calls

Pro Tip: Treat every new online connection - even if charming, attractive, or helpful - as *potentially fake until proven real*.

A Red Flag From Real Scams

Very often criminals will go out of their way to build your trust and draw you further in to their scam. Over and over again, I see cases where the scammers are sending photos of "their own" **(fake) identity documents, such as passports and driving licences**, to the victim as proof that they are a real person and can be trusted.

Ask yourself, why would somebody in a company be sending you their personal, sensitive, identity documents? They wouldn't - it just doesn't happen in a genuine situation. **It's a trick to build your trust.**

Usually the fake documents are well put together, but with a bit of investigation the validity of the identity documents can usually be confirmed. Below are mock-ups of passports used in two completely seperate cases, sent by different scammers. **Do you notice any similarities between them?**

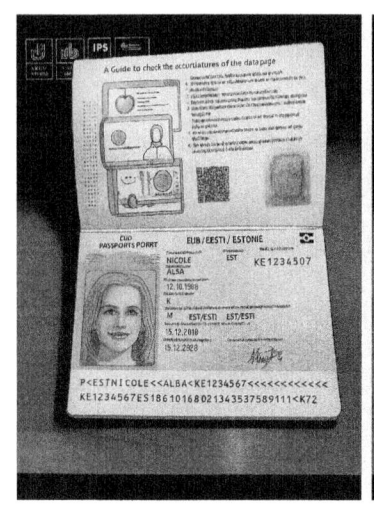

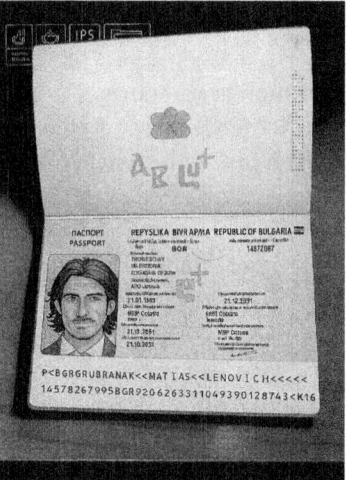

Hopefully you've spotted the obvious similarities. Both passports are resting on the same desk and black laptop and they are identically aligned - and also, but not shown here, in the original photos there is an identical shadow of a hand holding a phone present on them both.

The left passport uses a photo of well the known actor, Nicole Kidman, and when I carried out a reverse image search on the face in right-hand passport, the results showed it to be a French model, who appears on multiple websites.

Whilst both of the original photos could have been AI generated, I think, because they are so similar, that it is more likely they have been created with a popular photo editing app, using a template that the scammers have shared between themselves.

The original photographs are on my website realorcatfish.com/books if you would like to see the level of detail used.

Future-Proofing Yourself

Here's how you can stay safe in the face of evolving scam tactics:

✓ Digital Hygiene Rules:
- Use 2FA on all important accounts
- Keep devices updated (Operating system, browsers and apps)
- Use password managers (and stop reusing passwords on multiple sites)
- Back up critical data offline or in secure cloud storage

✓ Mental Hygiene:
- Be aware of emotional manipulation
- Pause before clicking or reacting to anything urgent or shocking
- Assume face value is fake - verify identity always
- Think critically about what people could do with the info you post publicly

Summary

Scammers aren't stuck in the past - they're evolving, learning, and leveraging AI just like the rest of us. We are approaching the end of the book, by now you should have a very good idea of how scammers think as well as how they operate and the

Key Takeaways:
- AI and deepfakes are making scams harder to detect
- Personalised phishing is the new normal
- Don't trust what you see or hear without independent confirmation
- Maintain strong digital habits and always verify

- The greatest defence in the future is not tech - it's critical thinking

In the age of AI-powered deception, your most powerful firewall is your brain.

CHAPTER TWENTY-ONE
Case Studies - Real Victims, Real Lessons

"The best teacher? Someone else's costly mistake."

Real stories of scam victims are a good way to **learn or teach**. Behind each incident is a person who thought it couldn't happen to them. In this chapter, we'll examine some real-world examples of online scams across different categories, analyse what went wrong and, most importantly, explain how each situation **could have been prevented**.

Why Study Real Cases?

- They highlight patterns used by scammers
- They reveal emotional triggers and decision-making under stress
- They show that anyone can fall for a scam - regardless of age, profession, or tech knowledge
- Raising awareness, they provide a blueprint for prevention

These stories are anonymised, based on verified reports, interviews, court cases, and news investigations.

Case 1: The Lonely Heart - Romance Meets Investment

Victim:
"Marie," a 54-year-old divorced teacher from Australia

The Scam:
Marie met "James," a petroleum engineer working offshore, on Facebook. He was charming, consistent, and emotionally supportive. After 2 months, James introduced Marie to a cryptocurrency opportunity that "his cousin in Hong Kong" was using to make huge returns.

She created a trading account on a website he recommended, transferred funds, and began seeing huge profits. Each withdrawal attempt required new "fees." Over 6 months, she lost **$247,000** - her retirement savings and a home loan.

✗ Red Flags Missed:
- James never video-called (his excuses: bad signal, busy schedule)
- He used stock photos from an oil rig website
- The trading platform had no official license or reviews
- All communication stayed on WhatsApp

Lessons Learned:
✓ Never invest based on advice from someone you've never met in person
✓ Verify websites - look for licensing, reviews, and registration info
✓ Romance plus urgency plus "opportunity" is a major red flag
✓ Always carry out a Reverse Image Search

Case 2: CEO Deepfake Voice - Business Email Compromise

Victim:
A financial controller at a UK-based energy firm

The Scam:
The company's accountant received a call from someone claiming to be the CEO, referencing a confidential company acquisition. The CEO gave instructions to wire **£243,000** to a "law firm" handling the deal.

The voice was perfect - tone, accent, even the CEO's sense of humour. It was an **AI-cloned voice**, generated from YouTube videos and podcasts. The accountant followed the instructions and wired the money.

✗ Red Flags Missed:
- Sudden large request with urgency
- Request to use new bank details outside the norm
- Call came from a spoofed number, not the CEO's known contact

Lessons Learned:
✓ Always double-check large or unusual transactions - verbally, face to face if possible
✓ Implement a strict dual-authorisation process for wire transfers
✓ Don't rely on caller ID or voice alone for identity

Case 3: Grandparent Voice Scam - "Grandad, It's Me!"

Victim:
"John," an 82-year-old grandfather in Canada

The Scam:
John got a call from someone sobbing: "Granddad, it's me… I got in an accident, they arrested me, I need $5,000 for bail…" The voice sounded like his grandson - but panicked and afraid.

The caller then handed the phone to a "lawyer" who gave instructions to withdraw cash and send it via courier. John complied.

Later, his grandson called - from school. He was never in an accident or in trouble.

✗ Red Flags Missed:
- High urgency and emotional manipulation
- Request to bypass normal legal processes
- Payment via untraceable courier drop

Lessons Learned:
✓ Always verify such claims with other family members
✓ No legitimate court or lawyer will demand couriered cash
✓ Scammers may use AI or social media clips to mimic voices

Case 4: The Fake Job That Stole Everything

Victim:
"Samantha," a recent college grad in the U.S.

The Scam:
Samantha applied for a remote data entry job on a major job site. The "company" did a text interview via Telegram and offered her the position.

She was asked by the "company" to deposit one of their cheques in order to buy equipment from a third-party supplier. The cheque showed as being "cleared" in to her account, so she paid the supplier. The "company's" cheque bounced a few days later. The supplier was fake and Samantha lost $3,400.

✗ Red Flags Missed:
- Interview conducted via text chat, not video
- No company email or onboarding paperwork
- Urgent request to process funds on the company's behalf

Lessons Learned:

✓ Research companies and verify any job offers through LinkedIn or direct contact

✓ Never deposit or move money for an employer you haven't met or verified

✓ Fake job scams are common - especially the remote, work-from-home roles

Case 5: The Tech Support Trap

Victim:
"Gary," a 63-year-old small business owner

The Scam:
A pop-up appeared on Gary's screen: "Your PC is infected! Call Microsoft immediately: 0800-XXX-XXXX." Panicked, he called. A friendly technician asked for remote access. Over two hours, they "fixed the issue," installed malware, and convinced Gary to buy a £299 lifetime service plan.

Later, his bank flagged suspicious activity - the attackers had installed spyware and tried to access his business account.

✗ Red Flags Missed:
- Pop-ups claiming your device has a virus are almost always fake
- Real tech support people never appear out of nowhere, unsolicited, like this
- The call centre aggressively pushed a sale on him

Lessons Learned:
✓ Never call numbers from pop-ups - close your browser and scan your PC
✓ Microsoft and Apple will never call you to report a virus
✓ Remote access should only be granted to verified technicians from trusted companies

The Common Themes Across All Cases

Emotional Triggers:
- Urgency
- Love or loyalty
- Fear or shame
- Excitement (too-good-to-be-true deals)

Communication Channels:
- Private messaging apps (WhatsApp, Telegram, etc)
- Email from spoofed domains
- Fake websites that look official
- Phone calls or AI-cloned voices

Tactics:
- Isolating the victim from others ("don't tell anyone about this")
- Layered trust (romance leads to investment)

- Realistic impersonation (CEO, grandson, recruiter)
- Untraceable money paths (gift cards, crypto currency, wire transfer)

How to Analyse a Scam Story

Use this simple framework to review and learn from any incident:

- **What was the initial contact made via?** Email? Social media? Phone call? Pop-up?
- **What emotional hook was used?** Love, fear, urgency, greed?
- **What was being asked of the victim?** Money? Info? Access?
- **Where could they have paused to verify?** What checkpoints were ignored?
- **What tools or behaviours could have prevented it?** 2FA? Calling them back? A Password manager? Critical thinking?

Summary

Every scam tells a story. And in each story, there's a moment - sometimes small, sometimes obvious - when a question asked could have prevented a disaster.

Key Takeaways:
- Real stories personalise risk - they make the threat feel real
- Most victims were smart, honest people who were emotionally manipulated
- Red flags often show up early - but only if you know what to look for

Learn from their losses so you don't repeat them.

CHAPTER TWENTY-TWO
Your Cybersecurity Action Plan - Staying Safe, Step by Step

"Security isn't a destination. It's a routine."

You've now journeyed through the scams, tricks, tactics, and traps that cybercriminals use daily - and more importantly, you've learned how to beat them.

This chapter is all about putting it all into **action**.

Think of this as your **cybersecurity checklist** - the essential practices and habits that will help you and the people around you stay safer every day, with minimal effort and maximum protection.

Core Habits for Everyday Cyber Safety

These are your "no matter what" daily and weekly routines - just like brushing your teeth or locking your door at night.

✓ **Strong, Unique Passwords for Every Account**
- Use a password manager like Bitwarden, 1Password, or

NordPass
- Let the manager generate and store complex passwords
- Never reuse passwords across important accounts (especially email and banking)

✓ Turn on Two-Factor Authentication (2FA)
- Prioritise email, banking, social media, and cloud storage
- Use an authenticator app for 2FA (e.g. Google's or Microsoft's Authenticator)
- Avoid using SMS for 2FA when possible (it's vulnerable to SIM swap attacks)

✓ Think Before You Click
- Don't click on unexpected links - even if they come from someone you know
- Hover over links to check where they really go
- If something looks off or urgent, pause and verify independently

✓ Keep Everything Updated
- Ensure automatic updates are enabled on:
  - Operating systems (Windows, macOS, iOS, Android)
  - Browsers (Chrome, Firefox, Safari, Edge)
  - Antivirus and apps
- Most updates often patch critical security vulnerabilities

✓ Use Trusted Sources Only
- Don't download files or apps from random websites or links
- Stick to official app stores or company websites

Monthly Security Checkup (15-Minute Routine)
Once a month, set aside 15 minutes to do the following:

✓ **Review Account Access**
 • Visit HaveIBeenPwned.com
 • Check if your email addresses were involved in a breach
 • Change passwords for affected accounts

✓ **Audit Your Devices**
 • Uninstall apps you don't use anymore
 • Check for any strange browser extensions or pop-ups
 • Review security permissions for apps (camera, mic, location)

✓ **Review Bank & Credit Transactions**
 • Look for unusual charges on your statements - even small ones
 • Report anything suspicious to your bank immediately

Set Up "Passive Defences"
These tools work in the background to protect you while you live your digital life.

✓ **Password Manager**
 • Auto-fills passwords and stores everything securely
 • Removes the need for weak or reused passwords

✓ **Antivirus & Malware Protection**
 • Use Windows Defender (free and effective) or a paid tool like Malwarebytes
 • Keep it updated - scans should run automatically

✓ **Browser Protections**
 • Install privacy extensions like **uBlock, Privacy Badger**, or **DuckDuckGo**
 • Use browsers with security-focused settings like Firefox, Safari or Brave

✓ Ad-Blocking
• Use an ad-blocker to eliminate malicious ads and tracking
• Use VPNs if you're on public Wi-Fi, especially abroad

Secure Your Digital Home
Some tasks for your whole family:

- *Teach everyone the basics:*
- "Think before you click"
- "Don't trust urgent messages without checking"
- "Never share login codes or passwords"
- Create a shared 'security conversation' - make it normal, not scary

Home Wi-Fi Network:
• Rename your Wi-Fi if it is not unique - don't use your name, phone number or address
• Keep your router firmware updated if it is not automatic
• Use guest networks for visitors if you can

Practice Scam Spotting
Run yourself and your family through the most common scenarios:

Phishing
• "Your PayPal account was suspended..."
• "Amazon: Confirm your delivery by clicking this link..."
• Look for:
- Misspellings
- Suspicious URLs
- Generic greetings ("Dear customer" or the first part of your email address)

Romance Scams
 • Sudden love from a stranger
 • "I need help booking a flight / paying a fee / crypto investment…"

Voice & Text Scams
 • "Hi Grandma, I need bail money"
 • "This is your bank. We've detected suspicious activity…"

Always **verify these types of contact through a second method / channel.**

Help Others Build a Cyber Safety Habit

• Share this book with friends, parents, and coworkers
  • Offer to set up password managers or 2FA for them
  • Help them spot scams in their inbox or social feed
  • Normalise asking questions like:
  - "Is this message legit?"
  - "Did you mean to send this?"
  - "Can I double check before I click?"

One conversation could prevent a devastating scam.

Know What to Do If Something Goes Wrong
 Even pros get tricked sometimes. The key is acting fast:

If You Click a Phishing Link:
 1. Disconnect from the internet (turn your Wi-Fi off)
 2. Run a malware scan
 3. Change passwords immediately - starting with email
 4. Enable 2FA if not already enabled

If You Gave Away Financial Info:
1. Call your bank immediately
2. Freeze your credit with all 3 bureaus - Experian, Equifax, TransUnion (US)
3. Report to:
 - Your country's cybercrime unit (Action Fraud in the UK)
 - The FTC (US)
 - Your local police (for a crime number and / or documentation)

If You Suspect Identity Theft:
1. File a fraud alert
2. Order your credit reports and get a credit monitoring service
3. Contact any affected businesses
4. Document everything

Closing Words: Stay Alert, Not Afraid
Scammers and hackers aren't going away. But neither is your power to defend yourself.

With every habit, every tool, and conversation, you:
- Make yourself a **harder target**
- Help protect your **friends and family**
- Can contribute to a **stronger online community**

Cybersecurity isn't about paranoia. It's about awareness.

It's about turning knowledge into small, regular habits - ones that give you confidence in a world full of digital risks.

Thank you for reading this book and for becoming part of the solution.

Printed in Dunstable, United Kingdom